interviewing

a practical guide for students and professionals

Daphne Keats, Conjoint Associate Professor of Psychology at the University of
Newcastle (Australia), has long been regarded as one of Australia's leading author-
ities on the theory and practice of interviewing. She is particularly well known
internationally for her work in cross-cultural psychology. Her many publications
include the highly successful *Skilled Interviewing*.

interviewing

a practical guide for students and professionals

daphne m. keats

Open University Press
Buckingham • Philadelphia

Open University Press
Celtic Court
22 Ballmoor
Buckingham
MK18 1XW

Loughborough
COLLEGE est 1909

email: enquiries@openup.co.uk
world wide web: http://www.openup.co.uk

and
325 Chestnut Street
Philadelphia, PA 19106, USA

First Published 2000

A catalogue record of this book is available from the British Library

ISBN 0 335 20667 0 (pb)

Library of Congress Cataloging-in-Publication Data is available from the Library of Congress

Cover design Di Quick
Text design Dana Lundmark

Printed and bound in Great Britain by
Marston Book Services Limited, Oxford

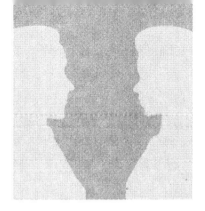

CONTENTS

CONTENTS

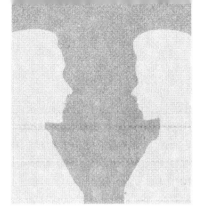

PREFACE

In writing this book on interviewing for students I have drawn on many years of conducting interviewing workshops for students in psychology and on many research studies in which I have carried out interviews myself or supervised others. Together with colleagues and students I have interviewed respondents of various ages, including children, adolescents and adults, and of many different cultural backgrounds in cross-cultural studies in Australia, the United States, Malaysia, China, Thailand and Japan. The insights which interviewing provides have never failed to interest those of us who work with this medium.

The book is designed as a course rather than a collection of papers which can be dipped into without reference to the earlier chapters. Chapters 1 and 2 introduce the student to the range of situations in which interviewing is conducted. Although most of the students who use this book will be in courses in psychology and the caring professions, I have covered in chapter 2 interviews in many other contexts. In my experience many psychology students do not become psychologists but can still use their interviewing skills in a wide range of occupations. The next group of chapters (chapters 3–6) introduce the skills which will be the main basis for all the following chapters. All these techniques—for developing and maintaining rapport, wording questions, probing and interpreting responses—which were covered in the earlier chapters will come into play as you work through the topics of chapters 7–15.

It is not possible in a book of this scope to cover all kinds of interviews and all levels of interviewing skill. For this, consult a volume such as Memon & Bull's *Handbook* (1999). There are also many specialised books on the more advanced levels of clinical interviewing; many situations in the organisational field could not be included either. This is not a book on research methodology, and it does not take a rigid view as to what is an appropriate method. One of the great values of using interviewing in research is that it can cross the boundaries of qualitative and quantitative methods, interweaving these as demanded by the data and the situation. Students should also use the book in conjunction with the style and content of their own disciplines.

The activities suggested are based on experiences in our workshops and in the research studies; so, I believe that they will have some practical value. The intention has been, rather than providing a set of prepared exercises simply to be copied, to design activities that encourage students and their lecturers to work up examples for themselves from their own experiences. The interaction of younger and mature-aged students can be particularly stimulating in this type of activity.

Many former students have told me how much use they had made of their interviewing skills in their later professional work. I hope that the students and lecturers who make use of this book will obtain as much satisfaction, and enjoyment, in putting it into practice as I have had with my own students, for whose work I have the greatest respect.

Daphne Keats
Department of Psychology
University of Newcastle

chapter

1

INTERVIEWING: WHEN AND WHY?

Everyone who works with people uses interviewing in some form or another. Psychologists, social workers, professionals in the many fields of the health sciences, counsellors in various fields, lawyers and reporters—all use interviewing as a basic tool in their day-to-day interaction with their clients. To interview effectively is not just a gift but a skill that needs to be developed. It can be learned and learning the skills of good interviewing while a student will avoid many pitfalls later on. This book is for students, to help them acquire those skills and to help them understand what goes on when one person systematically asks questions of another.

What is there in an interview that makes it different from a conversation? An interview is a controlled situation in which one person, the interviewer, asks a series of questions of another person, the respondent. It is possible, however, for more than one person to be asking the questions, as in the case where there is a panel of interviewers, or for more than one person to be the respondent, as in the case where the interview is with a delegation. The interviewer is in charge of the direction of the questions, which the respondent agrees to answer. The degree to which the situation is controlled varies greatly according to the purpose to be served. In this book the student will be introduced to a variety of situations in which interviews may be used.

Interviewing is certainly a popular activity. On television and radio, in news reports, in newspaper and magazine features interviews are daily reported—with politicians, pop stars, sportspeople and protest groups as their frequent targets. Students also have many situations in which they need to use interviewing. If you are planning to carry out a research project, large or small, you will probably have to ask questions of someone. Or it may be that your plan is for an experimental study to be carried out in a laboratory. How do you ask a person to become a 'subject'? How do you explain the purpose of the experiment in such a way that both the subject's role and yours are understood and accepted? How do you debrief your subjects after their task is completed? Those situations are as much an interview as a laboratory activity, and the laboratory task will not succeed if you fail to create a favourable relationship between the experimenter and the subjects.

It may be that your project requires you to administer a psychological test or a standardised scale such as an attitude scale. How do you obtain your subject's participation in a way that encourages the subject to willingly cooperate and put in the effort needed? How will you explain what your project is all about without creating a bias, or indicating your personal feelings about that person's responses?

It may be that testing and laboratory tasks both occur in the same project. Experimenters and testers do not always realise that their contact with their subjects is a form of interview, in which, from the subject's point of view, the test or experimental task is only one part of the whole experience.

In the laboratory situation the information the researcher needs is embedded in the responses to the demands of the task. It is often measured in terms of performance criteria as dependent variables, with background information such as age, gender, socio-economic status, and so on, treated as independent variables. When the interview is the main source of the data, the responses also determine the nature of the data but the range of possible response categories can be much more extensive.

In the interview situation the researcher must rely on the willingness of the 'subject' to answer the set of questions which the researcher has made up to meet his or her particular needs. How do you ensure that the questions asked are the relevant ones? How do you create an atmosphere which will encourage, but not bias, answers to your questions?

Perhaps your interest lies in the practical applications of your field rather than in laboratory experiments or individual research projects. It may be that you are planning to enter one of the professions in which you will need to interview people as part of your daily work role. The professional contexts in which interviewing has an important place are many and varied, and some of the most frequent are set out in chapter 2.

In this book we will show students how to make the most effective use of interviewing in these different situations. The book is intended as a practical guide for students to get them started in the right directions, but may also be useful for those who have to do interviewing as part of their work but need to improve their skills or have not participated in a training program.

As it is intended for teaching and learning, the book contains some practical activities to try out for oneself or in a group or class. Some excerpts from actual interviews are also included to provide the reader with some examples to criticise and evaluate. Of course, the names and places have been changed to preserve anonymity.

One feature of the book is its treatment of the role of cultural factors. In most countries today society is not culturally homogeneous, and in Australia over a hundred different cultural groups can be found and over a hundred different languages are spoken. This variety of cultural backgrounds can be quite challenging for those who must work with people from cultures different from their own. In this book we will try to show students how to deal with such challenges and how to recognise the cultural components in interview situations.

Why interview?

What are the differences between interviewing and other methods of asking questions? Many standardised psychological tests and scales are used in research and individual work with clients. Why then would you choose an interview when a ready-made set of items with a prescribed method of scoring the responses is available? Is one method more valid, more reliable, more objective? These are issues which will be discussed further in later chapters (see chapters 4–7). Suffice it to say for now that each has its proper place.

Where the users are competent to do so, they can use the testing and the interview methods in conjunction with each other. The special quality of the interview is that it is designed for a specific purpose. It is the particular group of respondents, and in the casework interview the particular individual, that is of paramount importance in determining both the content and the style of the interview. An interview can take account of many characteristics of the respondents which may not have been relevant to the construction of the standardised scale. Language and cultural background are but two of the important variables to be accounted for.

A feature of interviewing which is different from the administration of a psychological scale is the opportunity it gives the interviewer to explore the reasons for a person's responses. Questions which were not understood can be rephrased, and reluctant or anxious respondents can be helped by being given encouragement. This type of follow-up from the original question is called probing, and will be dealt with at length later. It is a valuable tool for all professional and research interviewing.

Another very common method of obtaining people's beliefs, attitudes and opinions is the questionnaire. Like the interview, it can be made up for a specific purpose. Whereas the interview schedule is designed for administering individually in a face-to-face interaction, the questionnaire is usually designed to be responded to by answering written questions. It can be given to an individual or to a large number of people. The respondents may answer the questions in a group setting, or they may be sent the questionnaire to be filled in and returned to the researcher. It is quite possible to include a space for the respondents to write in their reasons and make other comments, but unless it is possible to follow these comments up at a later date, the researcher is not able to obtain any further information or clarification of the respondents' opinions. Many respondents do not make use of the opportunity to add further comments because they find it difficult to express their ideas succinctly or because they want to complete the questionnaire as quickly as possible, to get it over and done with.

One of the greatest problems with the use of the postal questionnaire is the response rate. It is rare indeed to have a response rate of over 80 per cent. Postal questionnaires may yield a response rate as low as 30 per cent. The problem of deciding why the non-respondents failed to reply then has to be dealt with. A follow-up may bring very few additional responses. How much reliance can one then place on responses which represent the opinions of less than half the target sample? Who replied, who did not? Would the non-respondents have different opinions from the opinions of those who did respond? Did the questionnaires actually get to the addresses used? Much effort, time and money has to be expended to pursue all this.

In the interview, by contrast, once the agreement to participate has been obtained, the response rate can achieve 100 per cent. A few cases can be lost during the data collection and analysis, but once the sample is obtained the attrition rate is very low. That is, of course, if the interview is carried out properly. This book will show how to make sure that precious subjects are not lost through poor techniques and how to combine the interview and the questionnaire in the one research instrument, with the advantages of both methods.

SUMMARY

This introductory chapter has established that an interview is not just an informal chat but a controlled interaction which uses verbal exchange as the main method of asking questions. An interview has a direction and a shape; it serves a specific purpose and it involves both the interviewer and the respondent in a dynamic relationship. Many professional situations involve interviewing; even laboratory studies involve interviewing to explain the requirements of the study to the participants.

There are important differences between interviewing and administering questionnaires and psychological scales. Because the interview is created for a specific purpose and for a specific individual or specific group of respondents, it provides an opportunity to explore the reasons behind the person's answers and to verify the reliability of those answers with further questioning. However, although each method has its place, it is clear that the use of a combination of standardised test, questionnaire and interviewing can be very effective in the hands of those with the appropriate skills and training.

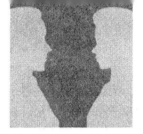

chapter

2

THE
MANY TYPES
OF INTERVIEW

There is a wide variety of contexts in which interviews are carried out and the purposes interviews serve differ widely within and across those contexts. Two of the examples referred to in the previous chapter—interviewing as part of a student's research training and interviews in the mass media—show how wide the gap can be between contexts and purposes. Between these two extremes lie many types of interviews: for social work; for clinical and therapeutic interactions; for counselling in many different situations; interviews in the organisational field for job selection and promotion, for performance evaluation and for dismissing or 'exit counselling'. In the commercial world there are interviews with customers and clients in many situations, for example in banks, real estate, insurance and financial management. Interviews in schools frequently involve parents, pupils, teachers, principals, counsellors and administrative staff. Police, religious advisers and the legal profession all rely heavily upon interviews to obtain their information.

These situations all require skill, not only to impart or to obtain the information required, but to do so in such a way that the clients or respondents leave the interview with the feeling that they have been treated fairly, that they have been listened to and understood. How often do people come away from such an encounter feeling satisfied with the interview process, even when the outcome was in their favour? When clients obtain what they want even poor treatment may be tolerated, but when the outcome of the interview is unfavourable the wounds from a poor interview become more painful. Bitter memories of the experience and distorted interpretations of what took place can ensue.

With all these different contexts and purposes to be served it is not surprising that different approaches will be needed. For example, if the answers to your questions are to contribute to a research study, you must not only be able to keep an accurate record of what takes place but must do so in such a way that the answers can be used later in the analysis of the results. Your data will need to be capable of as rigorous an analysis as occurs with any other research method which collects people's opinions, attitudes and values. Research interviews are the means to the end rather than the end itself.

In contrast, for the professional interviewer in the television and radio media, the interview itself is the culmination. All the preparatory work is done beforehand, often with the help of a team of support staff, and the few minutes available on air means that these constraints can cut off the conversation when that time is up. It is a common experience to have watched or listened to an interview which is cut off abruptly because the interviewer is out of time. This is especially frustrating when, after a slow start, the 'meat' of the interview is at last beginning to be revealed. A most important skill in the media interviewer's repertoire is to work the key questions into the brief time-slot available.

The research interview and the media interview have one thing in common, and that is that the purpose of the interview is not to change the respondent's attitudes and behaviour but to reveal it. Many types of interview also have that characteristic, but in others the interview is an integral component in a process of change. At times the line dividing these essentially different purposes is a very fine one. The mere experience of taking part in an opinion-seeking interaction between two people can be sufficient to change a person's views and subsequent behaviour. As the interview develops, it can reveal aspects of the topic which the respondent had not previously considered; so a change can occur even though it was not intended.

However, interviews such as those used in counselling are usually an important part of the therapeutic change process, in which the counsellors gradually help their clients to see things differently, and to confront their problems with a view to finding better ways of dealing with them. Such interviews can stand alone as a single episode but more often will form part of a total program involving several interviews.

Casework is the general term for professional work which involves dealing with people. As a category, casework includes clinical psychology and counselling, nursing, social work with clients, giving assistance and advice in employment agencies, community welfare services, police interviews, juvenile and court counselling, family services and work with the elderly. This list is far from complete. All of these types of work involve the use of interviewing as a basic tool for obtaining necessary information from clients. There may be only one interview; or a series of interviews may extend over a long period of time. In the latter case the same interviewer or caseworker may not be retained over the whole period for the same client. The reasons for such changes are many and varied, and may have more to do with personnel and bureaucratic or political changes within the agency than with the relationships between caseworker and the client.

In all casework records have to be kept. The use of such records will vary, and confidentiality (or lack of it) may become an issue, with serious implications. The culture of the organisation will be an important factor in determining what records are to be kept, who can demand them, and what degree of confidentiality can be guaranteed or maintained.

The context of the interview will also determine the nature of the content and style to be used. Within each interview there may be a number of sections, each of which may require a different treatment. Also, as will be shown in later chapters, the relationship between interviewer and respondent, or between caseworker and client, can change as the interview develops, requiring different techniques to be effective.

Box 2.1 lists many of the common types of interview situation. They can be roughly divided into two main groups: those which seek information but do not have the purpose of changing a person's behaviour; those which are linked in some way to an expectation of change in the person. The difference is important for both interviewer and respondent.

What many do not realise is that the 'fact-finding' interview, the research interview, over-the-counter form-filling exchanges, and even the background briefing to a laboratory experiment can all have an effect on the person's behaviour. And this is true for both the respondent and the interviewer. A 'good' experience can change the respondent's attitude to the content of the questioning and to the interviewer, and hence to the outcome. A 'bad' experience not only sours attitudes to the present situation, but these attitudes can also carry over to any future similar situations.

This subjective evaluation can vary with the individual: all people do not categorise the same situations in the same way. The judgement of one respondent may be based on the emotional impact of the interviewer; for

Box 2.1
INTERVIEWS ARE OF MANY KINDS AND TAKE PLACE IN
MANY SETTINGS

Over-the-counter information
services

Advice bureaux

At the bank

At the insurance agency

Tourism and travel services

Opinion polls

Telephone interviews
—surveys
—selling

At the school

Mass media interviews
—on television
—on radio
—in newspapers and magazines

Job interviews
—for selection
—for progress evaluation
—for retrenchment

Counselling interviews
—counselling for students
—marriage guidance
  counselling
—drug and alcohol counselling
—trauma counselling
—court counselling
—legal advice

Police interviews

Welfare service interviews

Clinical interviews
—hospital, medical, paramedical
  and nursing interviews

The cognitive interview

Research interviews

Interviews to obtain participants
in laboratory studies

another respondent it may be based on the perceived purpose of the interview, which also is subjectively evaluated; for another respondent it may be
based on the interview's outcome. The 'good' or 'bad' experience affects the
interviewer in the same way. Research interviewers who have to collect their
data from a number of respondents need to be constantly aware of the possible biases which may creep into later sections of an interview and into later
interviews in their schedule after a 'good' or a 'bad' start. Later chapters will
show how to deal with this problem.

So far it has been indicated that the many kinds of interview and the different settings in which interviews take place require different methods. Let us look more closely now at the special characteristics of those listed in box 2.1.

Over-the-counter information services

This type of interview, in which people obtain, or give information, is in one sense the simplest form of interview. The encounter is usually quite brief and the number of questions relatively few. It is usually confined to responses to specific requests. Typical situations are the information counters at shopping malls, at bus and railway stations, and airline desks, at enquiry desks in large organisations such as universities, local councils and government offices.

The usual feature of these interviews is that the enquirer wants to obtain specific information which is in the hands of the informant. At first the relationship between interviewer and respondent may appear to be the reverse of the usual relationship in other types of interview in that it is the person enquiring who asks the question and the informant who supplies the answers. However, the relationship changes when the informant begins to ask further questions and the situation develops into an interaction between the two people in which the possessor of the information becomes the expert in control of the conversation. This shift may or may not be favourable to the enquirer. It can be favourable when the expert becomes actively involved in helping, but can become unfavourable, annoying and frustrating to the enquirer if the informant is unhelpful, appears uninterested, or is impolite.

There is an inequality in the relationship, which has its basis in the ownership of the knowledge. It is exacerbated when the enquirer is poorly treated. What should begin as a situation of equal-to-equal social politeness can deteriorate to a situation of inequality, in which the enquirer is made to feel inferior. The language used, the non-verbal expressions, and the attention or lack of it given to the enquirer all contribute to the impressions given out.

Advice bureaux

Similar to over-the-counter interviews, but more intensive, are the interviews in which more extensive advice is required. Examples can be found in interviews with insurance agencies, banks, local councils, employment agencies and social service bureaux.

The typical structure is that the enquirer makes an appointment to see a certain officer of the agency, who has an advisory role representing the agency or organisation. Relevant back-up material—for example, the rules and regulations relating to the issue—is consulted, and the expert opinion is conveyed to the enquirer, who becomes a client in the process. The big difference between this situation and over-the-counter interviews is in the amount of personal information which is obtained and committed to file. Name, address, occupation, and many other details are recorded, whereas over-the-counter the enquirer can remain anonymous.

The change from anonymity to identity is an important one, especially when files are to be kept. The relationship between enquirer and adviser becomes more formal. Establishing the purpose of the enquiry becomes an integral aspect of the interview. It is quite possible, therefore, for the perceived purpose of the interview to be differently interpreted by the two persons, and this can be reflected in the way in which the interview is conducted and their different reactions to the questions and responses. Such discrepancies in perception may be consciously intentional. More often, perhaps, they can arise from cognitive failures in understanding; from prejudice, overt and covert; as well as from the environment's emotional effects upon the enquirer, which may be felt as a sense of being intimidated by the setting.

The requirements of this situation meet the more formal characteristics of an interview as the enquirer becomes the respondent to a series of questions put by the expert adviser, who thereby takes on the role of the interviewer. These interviews may be of any length—according to the time needed to deal with the issue or, alternatively, according to a fixed time-limit imposed by the adviser or the organisation for such interviews. There can be more than one interview on the issue, with several making up the series.

Tourism and travel services

Interviews are the most common method of arranging travel programs. Whether for business or pleasure, travel is increasing both domestically and internationally. The travel agent's task is to spend time finding out the client's needs, relating these as far as possible to the available hotel, bus, train and airline services, confirming these arrangements with the client, making the bookings and explaining the arrangements to the client.

Although computer-based communication has largely replaced much written correspondence and telephone calls, the process still involves much interpersonal interaction. Hotel and motel bookings, travel arrangements and connections all have to be co-ordinated to the satisfaction of the client. There may also be special needs which have to be taken care of, such as dietary needs and requirements for the handicapped.

Within the tourism industry many staff in the hotels and motels are also engaged in interviews with their guests. The success of the staff in coping with both easy and difficult clients contributes greatly to the satisfaction of both the guests and the management.

The structure of these interviews can vary greatly—from the brief computerised booking to long discussions with clients involving possible places to go for extended holiday travel, how to get there, what to eat, wear and do when there, what to insure against and what health measures to take. It may also be necessary to negotiate visas. With pleasure in prospect, the degree of satisfaction with the interview will greatly depend on how true and reliable the information turned out to be.

The relationships in this field are, therefore, highly personal and the success of the travel and hotel service interviews will be to a large extent dependent upon the degree of goodwill built up between the agent or staff interviewer and the clients.

Opinion polls

An opinion poll represents a very common form of the use of the interview. Political forecasting makes much use of the opinion poll. Many large commercial organisations use it, too, to obtain customer reactions to their products, under the general umbrella of market research. It is also used for surveys of people's attitudes to proposed changes affecting their lifestyles: for example, the pollster may approach people in their homes to seek opinions about the intention to sell off blocks of land in the area in ways contrary to current planning policies. Sales promotions of all kinds of products also frequently masquerade as opinion polls.

The methods employed in polling have a strong emphasis on the sampling techniques. The statistical analysis used in the treatment of the results flows from the nature and size of the samples obtained.

Telephone interviewing

This group includes interviews covering a range of different styles and purposes, employing a wide range of techniques. Both the information enquiry and the advice-seeking interviews can be carried out over the telephone. Much of the tourist agent's work involves the telephone. Many opinion polls are carried out by interviewing over the telephone, the political opinion polls being some of the most well-known.

Another type of telephone interview is the one in which people in distress seek help to solve their problems or to experience relief by expressing their difficulties to an anonymous, sympathetic listener.

These very different situations call for quite different approaches and we shall deal with each more fully in later chapters. The common feature of all telephone interviews is that the communication between interviewer and respondent is oral. Reactions are inferred from tone of voice, speech style and speed of response; but no non-verbal cues derived from facial expression and posture can be used to assess the impact of the questions or the replies.

At the school

A school interview is a situation familiar to all children, teachers and parents. Although so familiar, it can be an extremely complex situation and one in which interviewing skills are very important. Relationships between parents and school principals can range from easy to extremely difficult. Power distance may be very great, especially when the child is in trouble, and there is often some difficulty in communication, especially when the parent is from a non-English speaking or different cultural background and when there is a difference in social status and language style.

The situation may also be one of great stress for either the child or the parent. Decisions made as a result of such interviews can affect a child's whole future.

These interviews can be conducted individually or with all parties present. The location of the interview in the school, which creates its own particular environment, can produce many emotive and intimidating effects for some parents.

A factor affecting relationships between teachers and parents is the age of the child. The atmospheres in pre-schools, primary schools and high schools differ greatly. Another factor is whether the school is public, private or based on a religious sect or denomination. Where the school is dependent for its existence upon the financial support of its fee-paying parents, the treatment of parents in interviews must keep that fact constantly in mind. On the other hand, where they do not have such financial power, parents may not feel that they have a relationship of equality with the school representatives. Interviewing in such situations of perceived inequality requires tact and skill.

Interviewing children in the school situation can have many different purposes. Interviews may be for individual instruction and discussion of a piece of work, for remedial work, for research, for counselling, for discussions about subject choice and career intentions, and, not infrequently, for disciplinary purposes. These situations differ greatly and the skills involved will be treated in other chapters. They are important for all whose work involves talking with children.

Mass media interviews

This group includes interviews on television or on the radio, press conferences, and reports of interviews in newspapers and magazines. Usually a staff member or journalist interviews some person in the news. Typically a politician, a socially prominent person, business tycoon, sportsperson, or other prominent person in the news will be the target. Or it might be a bystander at the scene of an accident, or a police representative interviewed in connection with a crime committed. Another approach adopted by the media is to stop a few people in the street to give their opinions on some topic of current media attention.

The talk-back radio interview is yet another type of media interview. The listeners' telephone calls to the radio station are monitored and selected callers are interviewed by the radio 'host'. The purposes of the talk-back interview are very mixed: on the one hand, it provides an opportunity for the exchange of information and opinion; but, on the other hand, providing entertainment out of provocative commentary on emotive issues often seems to have a higher priority.

The purposes of the mass media interviews shift between informing and entertaining. When used to provide opportunities for political discussion, they are seldom merely informative. Bias is a common ingredient, whether encouraged or attacked, which creates arousal and involvement in the viewers or listeners.

Because television and radio interviews all have to be fitted into the time constraints set by the programs, the interviewers' skill lies in producing the most entertaining or provocative few minutes at their disposal while still being informative. The skilled interviewer can do this in a live-to-air interview. However, a media interview which was pre-recorded can be like the tip of an iceberg: by the time it comes to air it may have been cut and rearranged so that the original interview of, say, half an hour can be presented in a few minutes. It would not be surprising if at times the respondent ended up disagreeing with the impression given out by the version of the interview that finally went to air.

Moreover, in television and the print media all is not done through the verbal interchange alone. In magazines and newspapers, illustrations in the form of photographs and cartoons create powerful images which can enhance or detract from the actual wording attributed to the interviewee. In television the interviewer can create a desired environment, hostile or sympathetic, cooperative, confronting or conciliatory, by manipulating the studio setting. Studio lighting, placement of the interviewer vis-à-vis the respondent, the type of furniture and the distances between interviewer, respondents and studio audiences all contribute to a desired effect. Even the clothing worn can be carefully chosen to create a particular impression. Open-necked shirts are for a casual effect; formal dark suits and conservative ties are for the authoritative effect, while suits for women interviewers are supposed to suggest efficiency. Props are used as signatures (constantly holding a clipboard, for example), and the musical background is also selected to contribute to the overall effect.

The discerning viewer or listener will need, therefore, to decide whether the interview is principally to obtain and disseminate information, to incite an emotional response in the listener, to attack the interviewee, or to flatter the image of the interviewer rather than to obtain information from the interviewee.

Job interviews

Job interviews constitute a very large group of interviews, which serve many different functions found in organisational and industrial settings. As the list in box 2.1 shows, they cover the whole process from applying for a position to selection, appraisal and departure. Much research in the organisational field has been devoted to these kinds of interviews. Chapter 8 will treat these interviews more fully.

In almost all these situations the relationships are those of inequality. Much of the literature on selection, for example, concentrates on how the applicant should speak, dress and behave in ways which will impress the interviewing panel. In the appraisal interview the interview is a kind of examination of the employee's progress and efficiency by the superior officer. In the departure interviews, the use of such terms as 'early retirement', 'retrenchment' and other euphemisms makes it clear that the person is no longer wanted. Techniques for dealing with this situation concentrate on softening the blow with smooth language, saving face and preserving the dignity of the one who is to suffer the blow. Emotional involvement may be high in both parties.

Group interviews

A group interview takes place when the individual is replaced by a group: in some cases the interviewers form the group; in others the respondents are the group members. Typical examples are the interviews by an interviewing panel and interviews with members of a delegation.

The interviewing panel

Selection interviews are frequently carried out by a panel of interviewers consisting of representatives of the employers plus a number of others. These others may be 'experts' in the field who are called in because of their reputation in the field, as occurs with many professional appointments; or they may be representatives of more junior groups, who have an interest in the issue, or who may have been brought in to ensure that equity conditions are not infringed. This can lead to a very mixed group membership of the panel.

In panels it is the group that has the role of interviewer and the applicant is the respondent. The selection criteria may be either precisely defined or vaguely set out in order to spread the net more widely. However, what is set down on paper may not be what dominates in the actual interviewing process. The relationship can be both satisfying and effective provided that the panel pays attention to its interviewing skills, even if the applicant is not successful.

The group delegation

A contrasting situation to the interviewing panel is when the interviewer is an individual and the respondents comprise the group. Such a situation occurs when a delegation seeks an interview with a representative of an organisation who acts as its spokesperson. That representative might be a factory manager, a politician, or the head of a government department; while a typical delegation might be representatives of a trade union, members of a community organisation, leaders of a particular ethnic group, or a nominated group from the student body in a university.

The trade and cultural delegation is a variant of this situation. Often the delegates come from another country, on the so-called 'fact-finding' mission, or members of a delegation from one country meet with their counterparts in a foreign country. Problems of cultural and language communication complicate these interviews.

There may also be more than one person appointed to receive the delegation, and the delegation may allocate roles to more than one spokesperson. At times these interviews can become highly confrontational and emotive, with each side on the defensive. A typical example is the protest group sending its representatives to meet with politicians and developers involved in the matter at hand.

Group interviews are also common in the tourism industry, where tour guides explain to their group such things as the next phase of the tour, the historical background to the scenery, conditions for the group's accommodation, and so on.

The focused interview

Another variant on the group interview, the focused interview uses a group to share a controlled experience and then respond to questions about that experience. Typically, the group is asked to watch a film or video, listen to a tape recording or watch a set of stimulus pictures on an overhead projector.

This type of interview has been used in much research. It has the advantage that all the participants see or hear the same stimulus material. The questions about their reactions can be asked directly to the group as a whole or individually. However, when the questions are addressed to the group as a whole, several problems can arise. To what extent are the opinions expressed influenced by those of the most vocal members and how far do they ignore the views of the more timid speakers? Can the interviewer maintain control over the direction of the discussion so that it does not drift away from the focus of the exercise? On the other hand, when the questions are asked of each group member individually the main problem is that of the time delay. If the group is small, this may not be a serious problem; but, if the group is large, intervening events may influence the recall of individuals and the strength of their opinions, as well as their general level of motivation.

If the research conditions permit, individual screenings can be used, but it may be that the group response is what the researcher is interested in. The two situations—individual *vs* group response—may produce different kinds of results.

The guided interview

Used in research in many situations, the guided interview combines the interview with a questionnaire, test or task. It is particularly valuable when there is a language barrier, and when cultural, educational or intellectual difficulties are present. The interviewee is provided with the questions and the interviewee and interviewer work through them together. As the interviewee and interviewer proceed, questions can be answered: to clarify points, to encourage and remove doubts. In a research situation the problem of 'over-guiding', and hence introducing bias, has to be addressed. In clinical situations the main problem is in pre-judging responses and hence misinterpreting motives and reasons.

The guided interview can be conducted individually, but can also be used with small groups. As with the focused interview, the possible influence of one member of the group over the responses of others has to be accounted for.

The group discussion interview

A group discussion interview is usually carried out in a more informal setting, with members of the group being brought together for a discussion on some theme of mutual interest. The interviewer in this case has the role of a group leader whose task is to set the structure of the discussion, and encourage all members of the group to participate. This method is used in group therapy but is also a favoured method among church and community welfare groups and of workers with adolescents.

Video or audio tape-recording is necessary if this method is to be used in research, to record the content and direction of the discussion. In the freer atmosphere some more dominant members are likely to speak longer and more loudly, and it may be difficult to prevent many participants from speaking at once on an issue in which they are emotionally involved. When the group members are chosen to represent opposing sides of an issue (as is frequently the case in the mass media interviews discussed above) it can become very difficult for the moderator (the interviewer) to maintain control.

The physical positioning of the participants also becomes an important consideration: whether seated at a 'round table', placed on opposite sides with the interviewer in the middle, or seated in rows facing the interviewer. Different psychological effects are created in each case for both interviewer and participants.

Another important issue is the size of the group. If the group is intended to be informal, the group size must be relatively small. At around twenty the group easily breaks up into subgroups; if there are over twenty in the group the situation becomes more like a performance, with the interviewer directing questions from one person to another, like the conductor of an orchestra.

Counselling interviews

Counselling interviews comprise a very large group of interviews, which are widely used by many professionals. They differ from those discussed above, in that there is usually an expectation of some help being given in a problem situation and hence some change in behaviour is hopefully to follow. 'Behaviour' in this sense covers attitudes and ways of construing the situation as well as actions. It may also be the case that the counselling involves some other person or persons, as in the case of family problems. Counselling interviews can be individual, but group interviews (as described above) may also be used in counselling sessions.

Typical contexts for such interviews are marriage-guidance counselling, family court counselling, drug and alcohol counselling, school and student counselling. Counselling interviews following a traumatic event—such as after a serious accident, an assault, a bush fire or when someone is present at the loss of life of others—are important in helping people to recover from their shock and face the difficulties of their situation.

Interviewing is an important aspect of all counselling. It is used to obtain information but also to help clients to express their needs, fears and aspirations in ways which will lead to healthy development. The counsellor-interviewer is non-threatening and supportive. There may be more than one session needed to deal with complex problems, so the relationship between client and counsellor can change as the interviews continue over time.

It is apparent that the structure of these interviews is likely to be more flexible than those other interviews described above. In the counselling context there will be much effort put into developing a good relationship between interviewer and respondent, and much probing of responses.

It is important to state here that this is not a book about counselling techniques. Counselling requires training; it is not for the inexperienced interviewer. There are many reference sources and the serious student of counselling will need to consult these.

Clinical interviews

Clinical interviews cover a wide range of situations and, like counselling interviews, are concerned with obtaining information in the expectation of some beneficial change ensuing. However, in some clinical situations the change may be the direct result of the treatment by the clinician rather than arising from the person's own behaviour and rethinking of the situation. Hospital, medical, nursing, psychiatric, paramedical and therapeutic interviews of many kinds fall into this group.

One important feature of the clinical interview is the need to obtain reliable information to work on, for diagnosing the patient's problem. Another is establishing a relationship of trust between the patient and the interviewer (doctor, therapist, or whoever it might be). A problem for many patients is the perceived difference in status and power between them and the interviewer: the all-knowing, all-powerful professional versus the suffering, fearful patient.

The reader will notice that in counselling the respondent is a client. The change to being a patient brings a change in the role of the interviewer, which signals a change in the relationships. In a counselling situation the client remains in control, whereas in the clinical contexts of hospital and surgery it is the clinicians who control the direction of the person's treatment.

The cognitive interview

A cognitive interview is used in situations of stress such as after a traumatic experience, with eye-witness accounts of accidents, crimes and disasters, and with children's testimony in family-related court cases. Its purpose is to assist accurate recall of events and the associated feelings and environmental context. It is relatively unstructured, relying on assisting the respondent gradually to reconstruct a difficult or painful memory. It does not of itself have a counselling role but the experience may have a cathartic effect. Evidence from research and the use of this type of interview by police in Great Britain indicates that it is a reliable method of accessing recall of stressful events (see chapter 15).

Interviewing for research

This section covers those interviews that are the means by which the researcher obtains the data required. Research interviews differ from counselling and clinical interviews in several important ways. First, they are not intended to be an agent of change, although participating in an intensive interview can alter a person's attitudes and later behaviour. The researcher must take trouble to ensure that the questions are consistent from one respondent to another and as free of bias as possible so that answers from a group of respondents can be codified in such a way as to be analysed effectively. Care must be taken to select the respondents according to clearly established criteria which meet the needs of the research plan. Except with longitudinal studies, the researcher seldom has more than one chance to obtain the answers.

Research data from interviews also differ from data from questionnaires and psychological tests and scales. The distinctive feature of the interview is that it is carried out orally, which means that factors relating to interpersonal communication become important. However, the interview has the advantage that additional information can be obtained by probing the initial responses. Reasons for the response can be explored and all questions can be responded to without loss. This gives a richness to the data, allowing many individual differences in opinions and reasoning to be uncovered.

The methods available are many, and combinations with other methods such as questionnaires and scales can be used. As was shown (above) in the descriptions of the focused interview and the guided interview, many different types of stimulus experience can be used in combination with the interview questions.

The research methodology requires careful preparation of the interview schedule and development of appropriate systems of coding categories. How to do this will be treated fully in chapter 7.

SUMMARY

The focus of this chapter has been on showing the many different contexts in which interviewing is carried out and the differing methods which serve the differing purposes of those contexts. From the simplest over-the-counter enquiry to the most complex of clinical and research interviews, all have in common a dynamic quality which comes from the interaction between interviewer and respondent.

Interviews are used in many different contexts and they should never be treated lightly; people who give time and effort to answering the interviewer's questions deserve our attention and respect. The relationship between interviewer and respondent is complex, as we will take up in the next chapter.

chapter

3

THE INTERVIEWER– RESPONDENT RELATIONSHIP

One of the most interesting, yet demanding, aspects of interviewing is the relationship between the interviewer and the respondent. It is a dynamic relationship which develops as the interview proceeds. It begins on the very first occasion on which the two people interact and can change in many ways before the interview concludes. This chapter will first show how to use this relationship in ways which satisfy the needs of both interviewer and respondent. The second part of the chapter will deal with ethical issues, which affect this relationship and the integrity of interviewers.

As you begin to learn the techniques of good interviewing you will soon become aware of the differences among respondents. There are differences, too, among interviewers and each can develop his or her own individual style. That does not mean that there are no basic principles to follow. On the contrary, the good interviewer knows and uses these basic principles in ways which respond to the particular situation.

The dynamic nature of the interview is true of all the different kinds of interview described in chapter 2, but there are differences in the way in which the relationship is allowed to develop. For example, research interviews require much more formal control over the manner of questioning than counselling interviews. In the research interview the relationship must not be allowed to interfere with the unbiased collection of the data, whereas in much counselling and clinical interviewing the development of a relationship of trust is essential to progress and so may take much longer than the development of good rapport between researcher and respondent.

Many factors contribute to the dynamic quality of the interview. In this chapter we will concentrate on the interpersonal factors. In later chapters you will see how you can use the form of the questions, their order, probing and other structural features to create the style which will serve the specific purposes of the different types of interview. We begin with the interpersonal relationships because these will influence those other structural factors. We will have to recognise, too, the individual differences between the interviewer and the respondent, which have to be taken into account in developing the relationship. Social, cultural, cognitive and emotional factors are all present and have to be managed effectively.

OPENING THE INTERVIEW

There are three major phases in all interviews: the opening, the development of the main themes, and the conclusion or release. What takes place in the opening phase sets the stage for what follows, so it is important to make sure that it begins well.

The interview actually begins when the interviewer makes the first contact with the respondent. If it is the interviewer who is seeking the interview, this contact may be in a telephone call, by personal approach or by a letter requesting the respondent's cooperation. Or it may be that the approach is made by the respondent, as in the case of the advice bureaux, the telephone counselling services and the patient requesting a consultation.

First impressions **are** important. Although the careful interviewer will try hard to avoid making quick judgements about others, the cues given by voice, appearance and various non-verbal behaviours are interpreted and influence the interviewer's attitude to the respondent, even though unintentionally. The respondent, who is not placed under the same constraints as the interviewer, may use similar cues to make judgements about the interviewer. These reactions occur in the first contact; it is then the task of the interviewer to build upon favourable impressions but to be wary of making false judgements on the basis of unfavourable ones or previous stereotypes.

Rapport

One of the first tasks for the interviewer is to develop good rapport with the respondent. 'Rapport' is the term given to that comfortable, cooperative relationship between two people in which there are maintained both feelings of satisfaction and an empathetic understanding of each other's position.

People are not always able to express these feelings clearly or fully understand why there is good rapport. They may say, for example, 'We just seem to be able to get on well with each other', 'We're on the same wavelength', or 'He/she seems to know what I'm on about'.

Rapport is a psychological state involving both emotional and cognitive processes. The emotional processes relate to feelings of well-being, acceptance and lack of aggression; the cognitive relate to evaluations and attributions which are favourable. Many observed behaviours go into these evaluations: they can be based on appearance, on language style and on the social and physical features of the environment.

The most important factors influencing rapport are the conceptualisation of the situation by the participants, together with what is conveyed to the respondent of the content and purpose of the interview. It also has to be remembered that an interview is a social interaction; because it takes place in a social milieu the cultural norms of social behaviour are involved. When the conceptualisations of the interviewer and the respondent correspond to a great degree, there is likely to be good rapport. However, the emotional component can either support or negate such good effects. Anxiety, fear and feelings of rejection and low esteem in the eyes of the interviewer make for unfavourable emotional reactions. Politeness norms can mask these feelings.

Cognitive factors in developing rapport: conceptualising the interview situation

The respondent needs to be told what the interview is to be about, the credentials of the interviewer, what is going to be done with the information, whether the interview is confidential, and, if so, how that confidentiality is going to be guaranteed. If the respondents are taking part in a survey, an opinion poll or research study, they need to know how and why they were selected to take part. Having a clear understanding of their role will help to create a good relationship which will carry through into the rest of the interview.

The interviewer also needs to have this same kind of conceptual clarity about the relationship. There is a need to know the difference between empathy and sympathy, between friendliness and intrusiveness, and between encouraging participation and promising rewards for participating.

Social factors in developing rapport

Most people want interpersonal encounters with others to be pleasant; they want to be liked and to be seen as likeable. Politeness norms in every culture facilitate social interaction and must be used to help establish rapport. Other social factors relate to the environment in which the interview takes place. Language use, appearance and clothing styles affect first impressions and evoke stereotypical attributions and, hence, affect the development of rapport. These factors will be discussed in later chapters, where practical ways of conducting the interview are suggested.

Affective factors in developing rapport

The role these factors play will vary according to the type of interview. Many interviews involve high levels of anxiety—for example, when the person approaches a clinician or counsellor in the hope of obtaining help to solve a serious problem. Anxiety often also occurs when the respondent, rightly or wrongly, perceives a high status difference between himself or herself and the interviewer. Anxiety often expresses itself in hostility and veiled aggression, as we will show later in dealing with the hostile respondent.

Interaction of cognitive, social and affective factors

Emotional aspects of the relationship affect the cognitive aspects in many ways. Anxieties can lead to disorganised thinking, forgetting of details and time sequences, and incompleteness of responses. High states of emotional attraction also lead to bias, embroidering responses, giving answers which the respondent thinks will please rather than represent the exact situation or the respondent's true opinion.

Social aspects are also influenced by affective factors, but can also be used to control affective behaviour. For example, politeness norms may be used to avoid giving an offending response, or social platitudes may be used to mask feelings of anxiety or hostility. If the topic is one which arouses deep-seated emotions, social norms can be used to deflect or circumvent further enquiry.

Introducing the use of recording equipment

If the content of the interview is to be recorded in some way, for example by audio or video recording, or if detailed notes are to be taken, the respondent needs to know what will be done with these records. Many people are very wary of tape-recorder, which may affect the development of a good relationship with the interviewer. It is important, therefore, to explain clearly what will be done with the record. Anonymity may be promised; but, if it is, the promise must be carried out. A practice run will allay many anxieties.

DEVELOPING AND CLOSING THE INTERVIEW

Interpersonal relationships in the middle phase

While it is important to get started in the right way, the good relationships have to be maintained. Things to watch for are the effect of the content of the questions, the order in which they are presented, and the presence of bias and of emotional and other threats to good relations.

The same three groups of factors—cognitive, social and affective—continue to be present; but where before, in the opening stages, the attention had to be gained, there is now the need to hold that attention. If the topic is of real interest to the respondent, this need is present on both sides. However, in some cases of research interviewing it could be expected that the interviewer's needs are greater than the respondent's. The initial reason for selecting that person as a respondent therefore continues to be relevant in the subsequent stages. If the questions are not seen to be relevant by the respondent, the relationship will quickly deteriorate.

Cognitive factors are inherent in the phrasing of the questions and the total structure of the interview (see chapters 4 and 5).

Interpersonal relationships in closing the interview

As the interview draws to its conclusion, the respondent should not be left feeling 'up in the air'—expecting more, feeling that he or she has been prevented from saying what should have been said. No matter that a good relationship has been maintained during the main body of the interview, if the interview ends without the sense of reaching a proper conclusion, the good will be undone. It is important, therefore, to pay attention to the way in which the interview is wound down, to give a sense of release.

Both interviewer and respondent should be able to go away feeling that they have participated in a satisfying experience that was worthwhile. To help create that sense of reciprocal satisfaction, the interviewer has a number of methods available.

- Alert the respondent that the interview is coming to its close.
- Thank the respondent for participating.

- Ask if there is anything further the respondent feels should be discussed.
- If the topic has been a stressful one, come to the end of the interview slowly with less-threatening topics.
- Allow time for the conclusion in planning the time available. Do not rush the respondent as if his or her time was less valuable than the interviewer's. Rushing the conclusion suggests that the respondent is only being used for the interviewer's own purposes rather than as someone who has something important to say on the subject.
- Keep the notebook open or the tape-recorder going until the last thank you has been said. However, some respondents who have been very anxious will only open up when it seems that it is all over and a formal record is not being taken. Do not cut them off but try to maintain the good relationship and record or write up your notes as soon afterwards and as fully as possible. Also check your techniques for ways in which you might have built up a better relationship earlier on.

EMPATHY, SYMPATHY AND JUDGEMENTAL ATTITUDES

In many cases interviewers have to deal with very sensitive issues. Interviewers, like all people, are not immune from reactions to other people's behaviour. Situations of extreme distress may evoke strong feelings of sympathy, while evidence of aggressive, unkind or illegal behaviour may evoke feelings of anger, disgust and strongly antipathetic judgemental attitudes. How can an interviewer maintain a good interpersonal relationship with a respondent who is perceived to be undeserving of favourable attitudes? How can a person in distress not be viewed more sympathetically? How can the interviewer keep an open mind in the face of judgemental feelings toward the respondent, whether favourable or unfavourable?

Such issues arise most often in casework interviews. They can present serious difficulties for psychologists and for social workers, for workers in prisons, for those dealing with cases of rape, child abuse and domestic violence, and in family court and counselling interviews. Research interviewing on many topics can also encounter these kinds of responses and reactions.

To obtain reliable information from the respondent, the interviewer may have to keep such judgemental attitudes separate from the relationship with the respondent. How can this be done? The answer lies in distinguishing empathy from feelings, whether they are sympathetic or antipathetic.

Empathy

Empathy is a cognitive process involving the understanding of another person's way of looking at the same situation. It is 'putting oneself in another person's shoes'. The effect may in some cases lead to a judgement involving less antipathy, but this is not integral to the concept of empathy. Empathy is not always easy to achieve, for it requires complex conceptualisation of behaviours and motives; but it does allow the interviewer a greater range and depth of understanding. As the interviewer strives to gain this understanding, the relationship between interviewer and respondent is likely to improve and be maintained from there on.

The development of empathy does not preclude the interviewer from making judgements, but enables the judgements to be made from a wider basis than otherwise. Empathy helps to understand the reasons why people behave and think as they do, but does not of itself either excuse or condemn. It also helps the interviewer to cope with runaway feelings and with reactions to unpleasant pieces of information.

Sympathy

Sympathy literally means 'feeling with', but in many situations comes to imply kindly feelings for a person. An important difference between sympathy and empathy is that feelings are an essential component of sympathy but not a necessary component of empathy.

Sympathy does not necessarily involve an attempt to understand a situation from another's viewpoint. Sympathy may be merely feeling sorry for a person in distress without having any understanding of the background to that distress. Or it may involve sympathetic feelings of happiness or even euphoria without any conceptualising of the reasons for those feelings. Moreover, sympathy is not always reciprocated, despite the semantic meaning of the word.

In many ways expressing sympathy is unhelpful for developing an effective interpersonal relationship in an interview. It may become impossible to maintain the relationship if feelings change because of information revealed in later stages of the interview.

Of even more concern is that feelings of sympathy can produce bias: in the content of the questions, in the way in which they are posed and the way in which the answers are interpreted.

Reactions to judgemental attitudes

If the interviewer shows feelings of antipathy towards the respondent the relationship will not be one that leads to developing or maintaining good rapport. Judgemental attitudes which are condemnatory also produce biases. Such attitudes become quickly apparent to respondents, who then react defensively. They may clam up, giving incomplete and inadequate responses; they may distort their answers to present a more favourable impression; or they may even walk out on the interview, accompanying their departure with offensive remarks.

ETHICAL CONSIDERATIONS

Whether in research or casework interviewing, students and professionals alike have an obligation to maintain ethical standards. These standards are usually set down as 'guidelines' or a 'code of ethics' for the profession. In university research such standards are those set down by the National Health and Medical Research Council. Commercial organisations may have similar requirements although these may be controlled, not by a professional body, but by the legal requirements only. There are also specific demands associated with the kinds of relationships typical of the field. For example, a psychologist's relationship with a client may differ from that of a lawyer or social worker, or an opinion poll interviewer. Despite these differences, certain basic ethical considerations apply to all interviewing if an effective reciprocal relationship between interviewer and respondent is to be developed and maintained.

First, however, it might be as well to be sure what is meant by the term 'ethical'. The Shorter Oxford English Dictionary defines 'ethics' as 'Noun, plural and rarely singular, (the) science of morals, treatise on this, moral principles, rules of conduct, whole field of moral science. Hence -al. adjective.'

It is obvious that interpretations of what constitute 'ethical standards' may vary greatly, among individuals, and across cultures and social contexts. The interviewer working within a particular cultural setting must adhere to the moral principles accepted by that culture. An issue of great importance in cross-cultural interviewing is, therefore, how to balance the demands of conflicting cultural ethics. To take one example, a Western interviewer may see no ethical problem in a male interviewer interviewing a female respondent individually in private, yet to many people of Islamic cultures this would be morally unacceptable. Even within one's own culture opinions may differ and may change over time. Ethical standards are not immutable, as history shows in every culture.

Credentials of the interviewer

The matter of the interviewer's credentials is an issue of particular relevance to opinion polls, telephone interviews and research, especially student research. It is also of importance when another professional takes over a case in which a former caseworker has developed a good relationship.

The most important ethical demand is that the interviewer should present himself or herself honestly. If you are a student interviewer you must identify yourself as a student, not as a representative of your university, college, department or future profession. A psychology student should not imply being a psychologist, or any other professional worker.

In student studies the credentials of the supervisor should be provided. This is a question of who takes responsibility if things go wrong. Most universities and colleges have strict codes of ethics which cover research, including interviews, carried out by students. If the code is correctly followed, the student is also provided with some indemnity against error. Learning a new and difficult skill involving contacts with people is likely to lead to some mistakes, and if this occurs students need to have some support.

With opinion polls, and telephone interviewing in particular, it is crucial that the credentials of the interviewer are able to be checked. The telephone pollster introduces himself in words such as the following: 'Mrs Smith? I am Joe Bloggs from ... and I am carrying out a survey on ... You have been selected randomly (or perhaps 'specially chosen') to take part in this survey ...'. How can the potential respondent be assured that all is as it is being represented? One way is for the interviewer to precede the telephone call with a letter explaining the nature of the interview, its purpose and how the answers will be used, and provide an address and a telephone number for a contact person who will be able to verify the interviewer's authenticity. However, many telephone surveys by interview do not do this. If asked, and only if asked, the pollster will give the name of a contact person who can be telephoned. But what guarantee is there that the person who telephones and the contact person are who they purport to be?

Some opinion pollsters conducting market surveys deliberately do not offer the name of the organisation or company which commissioned the survey. As the commissioning company uses the responses to such surveys to boost sales of its products, the respondents could be justified in asking for payment for their valuable opinions.

In all cases of face-to-face interviews the interviewer should have at hand a clear, and verifiable, statement indicating the interviewer's identity, role, who is responsible and how the interviewer's credentials can be checked.

Promises of anonymity

The promise of anonymity is often made in opinion polls and in research interviewing. It can be appealing to both interviewer and respondent as it suggests that the respondent will be freer in voicing opinions, and have nothing to fear from voicing them. However, to offer anonymity is easier than to maintain it.

First, consider whether a promise of anonymity is justified. What difference would it make if names were used or withheld?

In research interviewing opinions sought may promise anonymity when the data could be used against the respondent. If promised, it means that no names must be used throughout the interview and no records must be allowed to reveal the identity. One problem with this is that the interviewer can easily forget that the respondent's name must not be used, and it slips out after the interview has moved into the main questions or at the end. The respondent may realise this only after the interview is over and the interviewer has moved on, with a resulting sense of being tricked and betrayed.

Suppose the interview is by telephone poll. No name is asked for, or used in the course of the interview. The interview is supposedly anonymous. But what other identifying information does the caller have about the respondent? Obviously a telephone number can be obtained from any directory and gives location of residence. What other lists did they have access to, in which the respondent's identity is known together with much other personal information. Such lists are bought and sold commercially.

In videotaped interviews in the television media it is a common practice to mask the person's face to hide identity. What anonymity remains? Voice, clothing and background setting all combine to give away information so that the masking becomes more of a dramatic device rather than a means of providing complete anonymity.

The ethical issues in these cases revolve around whether harm will be done by divulging the person's identity, and whether the sense of greater freedom to express one's views anonymously gives more valid and reliable information than if the person's identity is revealed.

Confidentiality

Another way of encouraging respondents to speak frankly on issues which affect them closely and to obtain information for which they do not want to be blamed, brought to court or punished is for the interviewer to assure them that what is said will remain 'quite confidential between the interviewer and respondent only'. What does such a promise entail in practice?

Like the promise of anonymity, the promise of confidentiality must be one which can be kept. Confidentiality differs from anonymity in that the name of the respondent is known and may be used throughout the interview, but the respondent is given to believe that the information given is not going to be passed on to another person or agency, or used by others, in any way which will identify the source.

To what extent can confidentiality be protected or guaranteed? There are many situations in which the interviewer might wish to maintain the confidentiality of the communication but legally it is impossible. Important and difficult cases occur when schoolchildren are involved: for example, a school counsellor is legally obliged to reveal information to the school principal and in any court case which arises involving the child. Cases of sexual and drug abuse are among the most sensitive and are legally required to be reported. Challenges in court to privilege have not in the past favoured those who have claimed privilege.

It follows that confidentiality should not be promised if it cannot be carried out. However, a serious difficulty can arise in the situation in which the interviewer may not be aware at the beginning of the interview that such information will be forthcoming. As the interview proceeds and the relationship between interviewer and respondent becomes more relaxed, the respondent may well become more ready to speak about something which is of concern, and, because of the promise of confidentiality and in a false sense of security, confides the information voluntarily. The ethical dilemma for the interviewer then is whether to inform the respondent at that time of the legal obligation, which will possibly destroy the good relationship built up so carefully, or allow the respondent to continue. An interviewer who puts a client's privacy and welfare first in this way runs the risk of a court subpoena and prosecution for contempt of court.

These situations can occur in both casework and research interviewing.

Care of records

There are various ways in which the information given can be treated as confidential and the names of respondents protected. One of the most important is the way in which the information is recorded and kept. Notes and casework records should be kept in a secure place. Filing systems should be kept locked. Many professionals avoid using names in personal notes lest they be legally required to reveal information obtained confidentially.

Computer records of research interviews can be kept confidential by allocating a number to each respondent, and keeping the list of names in a secure place separate from the lists in which the numbers appear. No other person should have access to the original list. In the case of student research, the student's supervisor may also need to be able to access the list. Respondents should be informed about what procedures are being adopted to maintain confidentiality when their agreement to participate is obtained.

When the researcher is reporting the findings, confidentiality can be maintained by simply discussing only the statistical results and their implications. On many occasions, however, the researcher will want to highlight the human experience with illustrations from the actual words of the responses and, for this, it is best to obtain permission to quote. If that is impracticable, then names can be invented. However, the collection of data may give away the possible identity simply by the way in which it is aggregated: for example, if only one location could fit the characteristics or if only a few people belong to the group represented in the data.

In casework the ethical considerations relating to records also concern the sharing of information, for example in case conferences. Professional codes of conduct bind members of those professions to adhere to the standards set down, but do not override the legal requirements. Students need to be very careful not to become involved in such issues, whether in their professional training or their training in research.

Truth in representing the content of the interview

This is an ethical issue which can arise when the interviewer is concerned that the topic is one which may arouse strong reactions, which may not be easy to cope with. To ease the situation, it is tempting to avoid telling the respondent precisely what the interview is really about. Examples can be found in those opinion polls which are disguised commercial surveys, and in research studies whose titles do not accurately reflect the content of the questions.

Apart from the ethical issue involved, deliberately giving misleading information also can have disastrous effects upon the respondent–interviewer relationship when respondents later begin to realise that they have been misled. It may by then be too late to retract what has been said but not too late to refuse further cooperation. An aggressive respondent could ruin not only the interview but also the tape-recorder or video camera.

Truth in representing the purpose of the interview

The real purpose of the interview should be revealed when obtaining the respondent's agreement to participate. For whose benefit will it be?—for the interviewer, for the respondent or for some other agent such as an employer? These are legitimate questions which the respondent needs to have answered.

The problems associated with offering inducements and rewards are relevant to this ethical issue. The 'carrot' may be too persuasive—the expectation of the reward may so cloud the respondents' judgement that they do not query the purpose of the interview.

Truth in stating the purpose of the interview is of particular importance in research, especially for student studies. Although it may seem to give a researcher greater status, the interviewer should not suggest or imply by innuendo that the interview is part of some grander research scheme when it is only a minor section.

Nor should the interviewer imply that the answers will contribute to improving the situation of respondents if in fact the interview is only part of an individual project, the results of which will be used in that person's thesis or university exercise, or possibly in an article which the interviewer will hopefully have published as the author at some later time. Although the topic may be important to the respondent, and results could be of value if they were to be utilised, there may be no guarantee that can be given to the respondent that this will be so. The actual likelihood of any outcome should be clearly understood at the outset.

SUMMARY

The aim of this chapter was to show how the development of a good relationship between the interviewer and respondent is essential for good interviewing, and how cognitive, social and emotional factors come together to affect that relationship. The importance of the opening phase in developing rapport was stressed, but the good relationships established at the beginning need to be carried on into the rest of the interview so that as the interview winds down to its close both interviewer and respondent feel that they have participated in a worthwhile activity. The difference between empathy and sympathy and how judgemental attitudes can affect rapport were also shown.

The second part of the chapter dealt with the importance of ethical behaviour—in stating one's credentials, in making promises of anonymity and confidentiality, in representing the content and purpose of the interview truthfully and in caring for records so that privacy and security are ensured. It may seem that this part of the chapter was more about what not to do than how to do the right thing, but taking proper account of ethical considerations is an integral part of building a good relationship between interviewer and respondent. It leads to trust, if upheld—and, hence, reliable responses—but to anger, frustration, lying, refusal to participate and incomplete answers if the respondent feels betrayed by unethical treatment. It is the interviewer's responsibility to develop and maintain rapport and to adhere to ethical standards. In the next chapter we will see how these relationships become translated into the wording of the questions.

chapter

4

CONSTRUCTING THE QUESTIONS

Constructing the questions is where an interviewer's creative skills come into their own. Not only must you develop and maintain the good interpersonal relationships which were discussed in chapter 3, you also have to put your questions in ways that will obtain answers. There are many ways of doing this, and you will see that the different forms of the questions— that is, the different 'question formats'—have differing implications.

As we examine the ways of creating different formats, we will also have to take into account the way the questions are worded, the language and speaking style in which they are expressed. All these factors come into play when a question is put. Our aim as interviewers is to have control over how they are brought together in order to produce the most effective inter- viewing technique.

The choice of format must meet the needs of the particular situation and purpose of the interview. Three major types can be found: open-ended, multiple-choice and rank ordering. Various combinations of these three types can be employed and within each many variations of format are pos- sible. What are their characteristics? What is the best way to use each type? What are their limitations?

QUESTION FORMATS

Open-ended questions

The open-ended question is the most common form of question in every-day use. Its principal characteristic is that it allows the respondent complete freedom to reply. It does not suggest answers or offer alternatives. It can be very general or very specific.

Very general open-ended questions are often used as openers and when a respondent is being encouraged to recall freely. They typically cover a broad range, leaving the respondent to take up a direction in the response. The response may then be followed up with more specific questions, depending upon the content of the reply.

Specific open-ended questions cover a narrower range; hence, a more limited range of possible answers is expected.

Experienced interviewers combine these in interplay, using one type to lead into the other. We will see in chapter 5 how this can affect the total structure of an interview.

Multiple-choice questions

Multiple-choice questions can take several forms. Their essential character-istic is that the respondent is provided with a set of possible answers and must choose the most appropriate or correct answer from among the choic-es presented. Students are all familiar with multiple-choice exam questions. Multiple-choice is also a common format used for opinion polls.

The principal limitations of this format lie in the fact that only the interviewer's choices are offered. To gain a little more flexibility, and to help maintain good rapport, a variant can be introduced asking the respondent whether there is any other choice, not appearing among the list offered, which more correctly represents his or her position. The new item is then added to the responses. This has the effect of rejecting the previous list, and so is not favoured in most opinion poll interviews.

Another limitation is that in an oral interview, such as one over the tele-phone, the respondent has to remember what the choices are in order to answer. If the list has more than a few items it is subject to order effects such that the first and last items are best recalled, while those in the middle are most often either forgotten completely or misconstrued. Opinion pollsters tend, therefore, to make their lists simple and short.

A variant of the multiple-choice type is the use of a scale which rep-resents positions from extremely negative to extremely positive. The word-ing varies according to the topic. The Likert-type scale is a common type of scale used in the social and behavioural sciences, especially in psychology. It is usually assumed that the scale is unidimensional and the scale positions are psychologically equidistant along that dimension. Usually an uneven number of scale positions is offered: five, seven and even eleven are popular. Names may be given to the various positions on the scale, for example 'always, mostly, not very often, seldom, never', or 'strongly agree, agree to some extent, neither agree nor disagree, disagree somewhat, strongly disagree'.

Leaving aside the meaning of the terms used for the positions on the scale, it is clear that when you have an uneven number of choices the middle category presents a problem. The middle position is intended to represent an opinion which is mid-way between the two extremes. However, respondents may also use the middle category as a way of escaping from giving an opinion, a device which in effect is a refusal to participate.

A more effective method is to offer a smaller number of choices with no middle position, thus forcing the respondent to move to one side or the other. This is usually easier if only, say, four choices are offered. People can say whether they are 'extremely for' or 'extremely against'; then, if they are not 'extremely' on one side or the other, they can say whether they tend more towards one side or the other. If necessary, their position can be clarified through further questioning.

Another problem is the assumption of equivalence in the scale distances. In research studies the equivalence can, and should be tested empirically.

A related measurement problem is whether the items form a single dimension or not. Multiple-choice questions are often made up of a number of components which are different from each other. Consider the following example.

These are some of the aspects of university life that students often talk about. Which of these do you regard as the most important to you personally?

a) Having a good library
b) Having access to good computing facilities
c) Many opportunities to meet with other students
d) Having good lecturers

In this multiple-choice question the respondent could answer orally or mark the preferred choice with a tick or circle. The interviewer could then follow up with questions about the reasons. However, there is no basis for assuming that the four choices offered would form a single dimension: whereas three of the choices refer to academic aspects, the other refers to the social aspects of campus life.

Another way of presenting the question would be to obtain an importance rating for each of the four choices, say 4, 3, 2 and 1, to represent 'highly important', 'quite important', 'not very important' and 'not important at all', respectively. This yields much more information than the previous format, but there is still the possibility that differences occur within each of the importance categories.

Ranking

If the respondent has to choose only one among several alternatives, there is an assumption that the others have been rejected. On the other hand, it may be that more than one of the choices offered is acceptable to the respondent. The question then arises as to whether they are of equal importance or some are more important to the respondent than the others. If the respondent is asked to rank them in order of importance, then the relative importance of each choice can be determined. Variations on the wording can allow for differences in the context. For example, if the topic is dealing with the frequency of a particular type of behaviour, the question would be expressed in terms of how often it occurred—the behaviour occurring most often being given the highest rank and the behaviour occurring least often, the lowest rank. Notice that, in ranking, the highest, most frequent or most important is ranked 1.

Consider the following example with seven choices to rank. The same four choices as were offered above are included, plus three more aspects of the student experience. Ranking of seven items is usually not difficult, but when the number of items is large (such as fifteen or more), the rankings are not so reliable for the rank orders around the middle of the range.

These are some of the aspects of university life that students often talk about. How important are they to you personally? Put the number 1 against the one which you think is the most important for you, then so on down to 7 for the one which is the least important for you.

a) Having a good library
b) Access to good computing facilities
c) Opportunities to meet other students
d) Having good lecturers
e) The student lifestyle
f) Having an active student union
g) Being independent

Note that there is no demand for the items to form a single dimension.

Combined rating and ranking

A criticism often levelled at rank order methods is that the same order might be given even though some of the items may be important and others not important at all. However, if the respondent is asked to both rank and rate we can obtain a better idea of the person's opinions.

The example in the table below shows how these differences can work out in practice. For convenience the same items as above are used.

Respondents	A		B		C		D		E		F		G	
	Rk	Rt	Rk	Rt	Rk	Rt	Rk	Rt	Rk	Rt	Rk	Rt	Rk	Rt
a) library	1	4	2	4	6	2	2	2	4	2	3	4	5	2
b) computing	2	4	3	4	7	1	3	2	3	2	2	4	6	4
c) meet others	4	3	5	3	3	3	5	1	5	2	5	3	4	1
d) lecturers	3	3	1	4	2	3	1	3	6	2	4	4	1	2
e) lifestyle	5	2	6	3	4	3	6	1	1	3	7	3	7	4
f) active union	6	2	7	3	5	2	7	1	2	2	6	3	3	2
g) independent	7	1	4	4	1	4	4	1	7	1	1	4	2	1

Respondent A is the only one who spreads the ratings out in the same way as the rank order. Although Respondents B and D give the same rank orders, their ratings differ, and while Respondents B and F are similar in their ratings they differ in their rank orders.

What can we make of respondents C, E and G? Both Respondents C and E are consistent in giving their highest ranking to the item rated highest and their lowest ranking to the item rated lowest, but in the intermediate positions the ranking removes the apparent equality in the items rated in the second position. Respondent G, however, is quite inconsistent, with rankings in the opposite order to the ratings. Something is clearly wrong with these responses and the cause would need to be found.

The two sets of responses give us different views of the respondents' opinions. If only ranking had been used, we would not have known whether these items were important to them or not, but if only rating had been used, the distinctions which two of the respondents were making would not have become apparent. The combined format also has helped to uncover the kind of inconsistencies which occurred with Respondent G. We can examine consistency between the rankings and ratings by converting the ratings to rankings with ties and then correlating the original rankings with the converted rankings.

The examples above are set out with numbers to represent positions. In framing the questions the interviewer can use phrases which have the same function.

Combining oral and written questions

An effective method of helping respondents answer multiple-choice and ranking questions is to combine the oral with a written presentation. This is a necessary strategy in research interviewing, in which a sample of respondents has to be presented with the same questions (their stimulus material) but it can also be useful in many other situations.

If the respondent is not familiar with the language, it will be helpful both to see and to hear the questions. In job interviews, and in casework, where reference is made to previous notes and various documents, both oral and written questions can be used. Another situation is in group interviews such as the informal focus group, where the group is provided with a list of topics to be discussed.

Probing

In probing, the questions follow up the answers to previous questions. Probing questions may be general or specific in format, depending on the nature of the original question.

Probing, as the term suggests, delves further into the response. It might be searching for the reasons behind the previous answer, it might be searching to resolve inconsistencies (as in the case of Respondent G in the combined rating and ranking example above), or it might be aimed at helping the respondent deal with a topic which has been difficult to speak about. Probing is treated more fully in chapter 6.

Probing questions can be used to rephrase the original question in order to clarify its meaning, using more understandable terms but essentially covering the same ground. Alternatively, probing can follow through with further, different questions, which are suggested by the answer to the original question. Sometimes they might refer back to answers to much earlier questions and can also be used to give feedback. Some typical examples are as follows.

Clarifying
— 'Can you tell me more about ...?'
— 'Could you explain a little more about ...?'

Seeking the next stage in a sequence
— 'Then what happened next?'

Seeking reasons
— 'Why do you think that?'

Checking consistency
— 'You said that ... but now you have told me ... How do you explain that? Can you tell me more?'

Revising
— 'Let's go back to what you told me before about ... In the light of what you told me later, can you now tell me more about ...?'

WORDING THE QUESTIONS

Whatever question format you choose, the questions have to be expressed in words which will be understood and will obtain relevant answers, which will not be ambiguous and will not offend. What are the ways of ensuring that your questions will succeed in meeting these criteria? Here we need to consider the language used, the politeness norms, and speaking styles. Ambiguity is found when questions are not precisely framed but also when there is more than one part to the question. Perhaps the most important requirement for meeting these criteria is to recognise and avoid the presence of bias in the question.

Bias

There is bias in a question when it is phrased in such a way that not all answers appear to be equally acceptable. A leading question is a biased question because it does not keep all alternative answers open. In its extreme form bias is a prejudicial attitude which influences the way in which questions are posed. It may be present in a single question, in a series of questions or in the interview as a whole.

Many of the common stereotypic views of people and behaviour are biased, ignoring alternative explanations and/or basing judgements on a small number of cases. Stereotypes are useful as short-cuts. Because we have to begin somewhere in dealing with a person we do not know, drawing on stereotypes based on what little information we have available can help to open up social interaction. However, they may also lead us into making assumptions which in the course of an interview may not be supported.

There is much research on stereotyping (for example, Haslam, McGarty, Oakes & Turner, 1993) showing how convenient and yet how misleading stereotypes can be. Stereotypes based on age, gender, appearance and socio-economic status are particularly common, but can be very dangerous when relied upon in interviewing because they lead to bias in both formulating the questions and interpreting the responses.

In this chapter we will only deal with bias in presenting the questions; bias in interpreting the responses will be dealt with in chapter 6. Bias affects the whole structure of the interview, in that a biased question may lead to biased and/or hostile responses, which then require further questions to overcome the unfavourable effects. It is the interviewer's responsibility to avoid bias, not the respondent's.

How do you avoid bias in creating the questions? How do you recognise it, in either your own questions or your respondent's replies?

Consider the following example:

— '....You do, don't you?'

Here the interviewer's expectation is for the positive response, 'Yes'. But what if the respondent does not agree with the implied behaviour? An outspoken respondent may simply say 'No', but another may say 'Yes', because it may appear that to say 'No' is a wrong answer, or that it would be unkind or impolite to disagree. To this respondent it would be more important to be regarded favourably by the interviewer than to maintain an independent viewpoint.

If the way the question is worded suggests that a 'Yes' is what most people would reply, the 'No' response may label the person as a minority, an outsider, with less of whatever quality is being considered desirable.

Expressing the expectation in the negative form has the same biasing effect, as, for example:

— 'You don't ..., do you?'.

Preceding the question with a phrase which suggests that a certain kind of response is what most people would say is similarly biasing.

To suggest that people with some desirable characteristic—for example, those that are sensible, intelligent, provident, attractive, mature, and so on—will agree with a certain position invites a biased response, as the respondent will hesitate to declare that he or she does not belong to that desirable category. Many variants of this approach are used, some deliberately as sales pitches. For example: 'Most sensible people who care for their future and those of their loved ones will wisely invest in 'Goldbest' shares. They're going fast, have you any of these?'

The desirable characteristic can be implied as well as stated explicitly. For example: 'As a member of [X] Church/Society, I expect you would be a regular attender/contributor. Is that correct?'

To avoid bias the interviewer needs to maintain an open mind. Do not preclude any response.

Bias can also arise when the interviewer makes judgements about a person on the basis of appearance, speech style, age and gender. Biased expectations occur frequently in dealing with physically handicapped people, who greatly resent them.

Ambiguity

Questions can be ambiguous even when bias is not at issue. Usually, careful wording can avoid this problem. Double-barrelled questions are ambiguous because they do not specify which part of the question the respondent should address. We will see in chapter 5 how this can affect the whole structure of the interview.

Whenever any ambiguity might occur, either from the use of a word or from the structure of the whole question, rephrase the question so that there is no doubt as to the intended meaning.

CHOOSING THE LANGUAGE STYLE

To make sure that you are understood by your respondent, it is necessary to choose a language style that is comfortable both to you as interviewer and to your respondent. You may have noticed in talking with friends how easy it is to use the same language style as they do, or when you are addressed formally by someone you tend to reply in a similar way. The difference between these two verbal interactions indicates a close relationship in the case of friends but a more distant social relationship in the other case.

In interviewing we want to choose language which creates a situation of trust, which is unambiguous in meaning and which enables the respondent to reply. We can adjust the level of difficulty in vocabulary according to the respondent's language skills, but some very common forms of language can cause problems. These include the use of idiom and metaphor, jokes, plays upon words, euphemisms, colloquialisms and fashionable jargon.

Idiom

Idiomatic terms and phrases are such a familiar and integral part of the language we use every day that we do not realise how unclear they can be to someone whose first language is not the same as our own. Even people whose first language is the same may have different ways of using the language idiomatically. Between Australians, Canadians, Americans from the United States and people from different parts of Britain there are many differences in the ways that idioms are used.

Although idioms are 'home grown', they are not the same as slang or colloquial language as they may be used in both formal and informal styles of speaking. This is called the 'register', and will vary according to the context.

Joking

Joking is often used as a way of relieving tension, of 'breaking the ice'. Some cultures use this social device more than others. Moreover, not all people see the funny side, even in the same culture! To enjoy a joke requires both speaker and listener to understand the point. Joking also may involve some kind of 'put down'. People who are sensitive to the presence of such a perceived slight, or who are feeling anxious, are insecure or are suffering are not amused when another person is laughing. They may feel that the joke is directed at them, or interpret the interviewer's attitude as not treating them seriously enough.

Joking needs a high level of established good rapport before it can be used as a language style.

Metaphors and similes

Like idiomatic terms, many metaphors and similes are so common in the language that they can be taken as understood by everyone. But, like idioms, they can be misunderstood by those not familiar with the language, especially if understood by their literal meaning.

Euphemisms

A euphemism is a way of avoiding the use of a term which might offend the listener. While the intention may be to soften the impact of the term, the effect may be otherwise. The situations most often eliciting euphemisms are death, sexual offences, sexual behaviour, terminal illness and misdemeanours of various kinds which are alluded to rather than spoken about directly. Some examples are using 'He's passed over', 'He's gone to his maker' or 'He's pushing up daisies', rather than saying 'He has died'.

Many euphemisms are used for the sake of politeness, especially where there are socio-cultural taboos about the use of the more direct term. This applies especially to sexual behaviour and references to genitalia.

Although the interviewer's intention may be to convey consideration for the feelings of another, the effect may be an appearance of prudishness or an unwillingness on the part of the interviewer to confront the reality of the situation.

Colloquialisms

The language used for informal interactions among people of the same background can be lively and expressive. But it may not be shared by others from a different background. Social class connotations may be linked to many terms, indicating a language style which creates a sense of social inequality.

When the respondent uses colloquial language, the interviewer does not have to use it, too, in order to be understood.

Fashionable jargon

This is the language which is used to indicate that the speaker is aware of the latest fashions; it is typical of the advertising media, and of cohesive social groups such as teenagers. It is often used as a way of identifying oneself as an in-group member. It often has a short life.

Because it is the means of communicating among group members, the use of this language style by a non-member has to be acceptable to a group member. It becomes quickly apparent whether a person using it is a member of that group or an outsider. When the communication is between persons who are mutually accepting of the others' right to use the in-group language no problem arises. However, when a person who is not a group member, such as an interviewer, attempts to do so in order to demonstrate in-group knowledge but without prior acceptance by that group, there will be resentment leading to failure in communication.

Moreover, the transitory nature of such language may make the attempt to be in fashion appear sadly and foolishly out of date. It is far better to use language which has a longer history and more general usage.

Politeness norms

Whatever format you choose for them, questions not only have to be expressed in unambiguous, unbiased terms, they also have to be spoken in a manner which is polite. What is considered polite varies greatly with the context and with the culture. The norms of polite behaviour are not so easy to adhere to in a heterogeneous or multicultural society. They may also vary according to the age group and social position, older and more senior people generally tending to have more concern for the norms and a greater expectation for their adherence than their juniors.

How can the interviewer use language which does not offend politeness norms? The need to show respect for others, whatever their social group, is the key to developing and maintaining good relationships with one's respondent. Avoiding fashionable jargon and using straightforward language are also helpful. More will be said on this issue in later chapters.

Non-verbal cues

Gestures, facial expressions and tone of voice all add to the way the words in the questions are interpreted and expressed. They act simultaneously with the language to convey our meaning. As interviewers we need to control these cues. They may express attitudes which bias the question because they convey an implication which contradicts the words; they can convey feelings about the respondent which can inhibit the relationship, or falsely flatter it; they can distract the respondent's concentration from the substance of the question.

This is not to say that the interviewer is to remain poker-faced, devoid of warmth and uninterested. However, it is important to be aware of the message that is being conveyed by means other than the words. See also chapter 6.

Voice

The tone of voice is often regarded as a non-verbal cue because the same words can be imbued with different meanings simply by the way they are spoken. Actors, of course, do this with great skill. Interviewers, however, may do it also—sometimes without being aware of the effect being created and sometimes deliberately. The tone of voice can turn a statement into a question, and a question into a statement; it can raise a doubt, suggest incredulity, agreement or disagreement—all without changing a word.

As with other non-verbal cues, it is important to be aware of the effect upon the respondent and to learn how to control this effect.

Speech style

Yet another aspect of the effect of vocal difference is that of accent. Clarity of speech is necessary to convey our questions, but there is no one accent that is the most desirable. The interviewer is most effective when he or she shows integrity in relations with the respondent. Part of that integrity comes from integrity in the way one speaks. Even if the situation may call for differences in register there is no need to try to be someone else.

SUMMARY

In this chapter we have concentrated on how to create and deliver the questions. A number of formats were shown, including general and specific, open-ended and closed types such as multiple-choice and ranking, and ways of combining written and oral questions. This chapter also showed how to recognise and overcome bias in constructing and asking questions, the importance of adhering to the politeness norms and speech styles which are acceptable to the respondent and yet retain the interviewer's integrity.

ACTIVITIES FOR STUDENTS

Using the same topic, make up questions in each of the formats discussed. What are the differences in the style of wording used?

Try out different ways of creating questions which are biased. Make up two versions of each question, one which is biased and one which is not.

chapter

5

THE STRUCTURE OF
THE INTERVIEW

This chapter treats the interview as a whole, showing how the interview develops as each question leads to a response and that response leads on to further questions and responses until the topic is covered. Within the total set of questions and responses there are many ways in which they can be brought together to form a cohesive structure.

Because an interview always has a purpose, it is important to create a structure which will help to achieve that purpose. However, the respondent has no responsibility to help achieve the interviewer's goals; it is the task of the interviewer to ensure that the purpose will be achieved, and achieved effectively. This means taking account of all that occurs, from the opening words to the final thanking of the respondent.

As was shown in chapter 3 in relation to developing rapport, there are three main phases in an interview: the opening phase, the development of the main body of questions and the closing phase. Each is important. The interactions involved in developing the good interviewer–respondent rapport and obtaining the willingness of the respondent to participate, which have to be developed at the beginning stage, all form part of the total structure. Similarly, the concluding stage in which the respondent is released from the interview is also part of the total structure. In between, the question-response-question sequence can take many forms. The questions themselves can be phrased in many different formats (see chapter 4).

In treating the interview as a whole we also need to consider the effects of the context in which it takes place. The context is both physical, involving the location and its characteristics (such as office, home or school), and psychological, involving the personal aspects of needs, coercion or freedom to participate. The contexts place constraints upon the use of many of the types of interview described in chapter 2.

THE OPENING PHASE

The interview begins with the first contact between interviewer and respondent. Much depends on how the interviewer represents the purpose of the interview and his or her credentials. Who is requesting the interview? Is it the respondent, the interviewer or some other agency such as the police, welfare agency or the court? How free is the respondent to participate or not? Whatever the circumstances which lead to the interview may be, it is important to establish the good relationship before the main body of questions is reached. Time spent on establishing rapport at this opening phase will not be wasted.

Establishing your credentials

In interviews between individuals who previously did not know each other, as in the case of telephone surveys, opinion polls and research interviews, it is important that the potential respondent be correctly informed as to who the interviewer is, what is his or her role/employer/affiliation, and so on. It is often tempting, in order to obtain cooperation, to make out that one has a greater status than is actually the case, or to allow the potential respondent to continue in a misapprehension which will enhance the interviewer's chances of gaining the interview. Opinion polls which purport to be impartial may not be merely seeking opinions but may be intended to sell a product, or gather ammunition for a political campaign. While it might seem to be an advantage at first to tell half-truths or imply a different purpose from the actual one, it will lead to anger when the truth is found out.

Students who carry out interviews as part of their training are particularly affected in this regard. It is essential that one's student status be made clear, especially if the interviews are part of a research or laboratory exercise. Do not suggest that your data will have benefits which may not eventuate.

Make sure that the respondent is told who is in charge as supervisor and how to verify your credentials. Fortunately, today, ethics committees in higher education institutions keep close guard over the proposals but in the field the student is on his or her own and must take the responsibility for any misleading information.

Introducing the methods to be used

The respondent needs to be informed as to what method of asking the questions and recording the responses will be used. What will the answers be used for? If a video-camera or tape-recorder is to be used, permission must be obtained. Allow time for a practice run. Respondents who are not used to being recorded may be nervous at first and may like to hear or see themselves. In some cases they may ask to have it played back at the end.

Respondents often want to know how long the interview will take. Do not deliberately suggest a shorter time than you actually expect. When that time is up but you have not reached the end, the respondent may simply decide to stop as they have given you the agreed number of minutes. We will see in later chapters the situations in which this is most likely to occur.

Obtaining factual background data

The opening phase of the interview is a time when much basic background information can be obtained. Not only does this help the interviewer to find out the essential background of the respondent, it also helps the respondent to relax from any initial tension as simple facts are provided. The interviewer should seek only relevant information. These questions also have the function of providing practice in responding and in the use of any recording equipment.

Combined methods can be used, with both oral and written questions and prepared forms for the answer.

CONTINUING AND CLOSING THE INTERVIEW

The main body of the interview

The main body of the interview develops the main themes and explores the responses with probing. In general, the topics move from the more general to the more particular, and begin with the least threatening aspects.

In the development of the themes the interviewer can make use of the many ways in which the questions can be expressed. There is a great degree of flexibility in this part of the interview. How the total structure is affected is shown later in this chapter.

The closing phase

As the interview comes to its close it should leave the interviewer and the respondent with the feeling that they have participated in something that has been worthwhile. A long interview on a serious topic can be very demanding and, indeed, quite tiring for both interviewer and respondent. Respondents may become highly involved, both cognitively and emotionally.

It is important therefore to ensure that the release is not too sudden. A more gradual winding down rather than an abrupt finish will leave a greater sense of satisfaction.

Thank the person for their interest and effort.

If the respondent asked to hear the interview played back, now is the time to do so. Many will not want to hear it all, but it is important to do what has been promised.

This phase is an important part of the total structure and needs to be included in the planning of the interview as a whole. It is especially important when dealing with stressful topics.

If the interview is part of a series and a further interview will follow, the link between this and the next will need to be established, although this alone may not be sufficient to leave the respondent with a sense of release.

ANALYSING THE STRUCTURE

The different types of interviews described in chapter 2 place different demands upon the interviewer and respondent and hence produce different types of structure. In some types the structure can be planned ahead, but in others, especially those involving probing, the structure evolves as the interview progresses. One of the most valuable skills for an interviewer is to be aware of the structure that is developing as the interview proceeds.

How can you as an interviewer keep aware of what is going on? Consider these questions.

- Do you know which way the sequence of questions and responses is leading?
- Are you on track?
- Has the respondent led you into a topic which you did not intend?
- If so, is it an intentional digression to distract you from your purpose?
- Have you simply forgotten your original intent and been led into another topic which seems to be interesting?

- How can you get back on track?
- Have you taken account of each aspect of a complex response or only followed up on one aspect and neglected others?
- Have you taken account of non verbal cues? Did they support or deny the words spoken?
- Have you remembered what was said earlier on? Is what is being said at a later stage consistent with previous responses? Does it add to, or explain a previous response? Or does the later response suggest that the previous one was not as straightforward as it might have seemed at the time? If so, how can you find out?

We can find answers to these questions by examining the structure of the interview as a whole. To do so as we go along is difficult at first, but as your skill develops you will become sensitive to these issues and alert to responding to them. So much takes place in a few brief exchanges that you will be surprised at the length of a transcription of even a few minutes' questions and answers.

The structure of the interview as a whole is composed of many substructures. These can vary and many different configurations can occur in the one interview, with strings of these substructures making up the total picture.

The question format can determine the configuration to a great extent; but, when the format is less constrained, it is the responses which determine the direction in which the structure will develop. It is neither the questions alone nor the responses alone but the dynamic interplay between them which creates the structure. We shall turn, therefore, to the various ways in which these structures are composed. The following configurations and examples are as described by Keats (1993, pp36–41).

Simple structure: independent items

The simplest form is that in which each question receives a response but there is no connection between the response to the previous question and the next question. The exchange can be represented as shown in figure 5.1. This kind of exchange is typical of the opinion poll or fact-finding type of interview, where there is a set list of questions and a set list of respondents but no personal involvement between the interviewer and respondent.

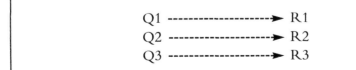

Figure 5.1: Simple structure: independent items

Q1: When did you come to Australia, Mrs A?
R1: 1954.
Q2: How many children have you, Mrs A?
R2: Seven.
Q3: What is your husband's occupation?
R3: Carpenter.

In the sequence in this example, question 1 leads to response 1, question 2 leads to response 2, and so on, but the response to each question does not affect the form of the next question.

Sequential items: chain structure

Contrast the previous sequence with one in which the interviewer adapts the question in accord with the previous response. This new sequence is represented in figure 5.2.

Q1 ------> R1 ------> Q2 ------> R2 ------> Q3 ------> R3

Figure 5.2: Sequential items — chain structure

Q1: When did you first come to Australia, Mrs A?
R1: 1954.
Q2: Did you come by air or by ship?
R2: By ship.
Q3: Did you like the ship travel?
R3: No, it was very uncomfortable.
Q4: What was uncomfortable about it?
R4: It was very crowded.

In this sequence, the respondent is being allowed to take charge of the direction of the interview. The interviewer simply goes along with the content of the response without intervening or attempting to check back on previous responses. This sequence creates a free-flowing structure. Such a structure has its place in situations such as the cognitive interview, where it is important to let the respondent use cognitive associations to recreate a situation in memory which may be difficult to recall.

Branching structure with channelling effects

The simple sequence structure can be effective when there is only one response to each question. However, if there is more than one aspect to the response, an interviewer might select one aspect and ignore others. The effect upon the total structure is to channel the interview in one direction only, as can be seen in figure 5.3.

```
            R1
Q1--➤R2                R4
    R3--➤Q2--➤R5
            R6--➤Q3--➤R7--➤Q4--➤R8
```

Figure 5.3: Branching structure with channelling effects

The following example is from a job interview.

Q1: What was there in your previous work experience which makes you feel qualified for this position?
R1: Well, I've had three years in personnel work,
R2: and we studied how to deal with these kinds of problems in the training course.
R3: I've also worked with computers before.
Q2: What computers have you worked with?
R4: Well, I've done most of my work on IBM
R5: but I've also worked with Macintosh
R6: and I've done a bit of work on the VAX.
Q3: Have you done any advanced programming on the VAX?
R7: Yes, in my last job I did the programming for three research jobs they were doing.
Q4: What were they?
R8: We did one on water usage.
R9: There was another one on coal fuel development.
R10: The other one was on coastal soil conservation.
Q5: What was the study on coastal soil conservation?
R11 They were trying to develop a model for drift in the high sand dunes.
Q6: Did they succeed in producing a model?
R12: No, I don't think it was a huge success.

It can be seen how easily bias can enter into the interview if this occurs. In this example only one aspect was selected for further exploration. Why that aspect and not another? Was it simply the first or last mentioned and hence the easiest to recall? Was it the most interesting or the most relevant? In whose interest was it to go along that path, the respondent's or the interviewer's? Was the interviewer avoiding a response which was not as easy to deal with, or has that path been chosen because it more closely accords with the interviewer's own views?

Moreover, we cannot tell whether there is deliberate bias or whether the interviewer is not aware of what is occurring. The effect upon the respondent may well be to perceive bias on the part of the interviewer, whether intentional or not.

Sequential structure with simple feedback loops

How can the interviewer overcome the problem of bias entering the interview? One way is to be careful to return to each part of the first response. This means remembering all the parts and using them later in feedback loops. Figure 5.4 shows what this means in practice. The structure becomes more complex and places greater demands upon the interviewer but is more satisfying to the respondent.

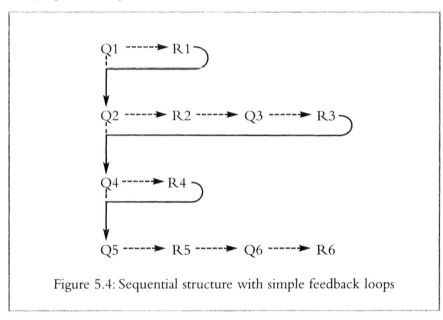

Figure 5.4: Sequential structure with simple feedback loops

The following example was taken from an interview with an adult male about attitudes to violence on television.

Q1: Do you think there is much violence portrayed on TV?
R1: Yes, quite a lot.
Q2: Do you watch any violent shows yourself?
R2: Yes.
Q3: What ones?
R3: Oh, I especially like to watch any James Bond shows.
Q4: Do you think there's as much violence on James Bond shows as on other shows, or do they have more or less violence than other shows?

R4: More I think.
Q5: What other violent shows do you watch?
R5: [names police show].
Q6: Any other?
R6: [names action-adventure show].
Q7: Any other?
R7: Well, not any other one regularly. If there's something on that looks exciting I'll watch it.
Q8: Do you think that you would watch as much violence as other people, less, or more?
R8: Oh, about the same I guess. I'm just about average, I guess.

Branching structure with complex feedback loops

This is the most complex structure. It takes into account multiple aspects of the responses at each step in the exchange; it returns to earlier questions and responses, relating later parts to earlier parts of both questions and answers. The structure is shown in figure 5.5. The example following comes from an interview on mother–child interaction.

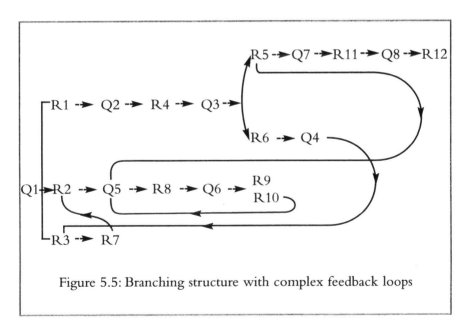

Figure 5.5: Branching structure with complex feedback loops

Q1: What do you usually do when Gary [the child] disobeys you?
R1: I usually speak firmly to him.
R2: Well, sometimes if he is really naughty I give him a light smack.
R3: If I have absolutely run out of patience, I send him to his room until he recovers.

Q2: What do you usually say when you 'speak firmly' to him?
R4: Oh just something to tell him who's the boss.
Q3: Can you give me an example?
R5: Well, the other day he wouldn't go to bed when it was time. I spoke to him several times before I got cross. He could tell by my voice I was cross.
R6: And I usually threaten to take away some of his toys when he disobeys me.
Q4: What do you say when you do that?
R7: Well I mostly say, 'Well, Gary, if you don't stop that before I count three that train (or whatever he's playing with at the time) will go straight into the cupboard'. And I do it too. Then I'd send him to his room.
Q5: Let's come back to the times when you'd give him a light smack. When would you do that?
R8: When he keeps on taking Peter's things. Peter, that's his brother. He's only little but they get a bit wild playing together and he won't listen to anything I say.
Q6: Who won't?
R9: Oh, Gary, Peter's all right.
R10: Oh yes, and when he gets into his father's tools and things.
Q7: You said he could tell by your voice when you are cross. How do you know he can?
R11: You can see by the look on his face. He looks sort of frightened and guilty. I always feel bad about that.
Q8: Why do you think you feel bad about it?
R12: Oh he's really such a little fellow,
R13: but you've got to be firm.

Although this configuration appears complex, in practice it is one of the most useful. It requires concentration to keep in mind all that is said and choose the appropriate time and opportunity to return to a previous question or response so that the interaction moves smoothly towards a full reply.

Constellated structures

With the possible exception of the just described branching structure with complex feedback loops, the other structures can often be used in constellations which are complete in themselves. The length of the strings can vary but are generally not longer than five or so question-response pairs. What distinguishes the constellations from other structures is their closure. When the set is complete, the interview may turn to another theme. Formats with multiple-choice questions and rank-order sets have this characteristic (examples being shown in figure 5.6).

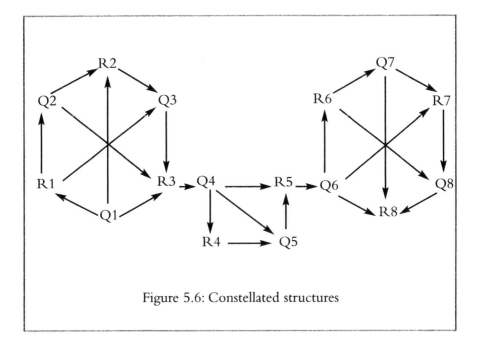

Figure 5.6: Constellated structures

Examining the structure

As the examples in this chapter show, even the briefest of exchanges can involve very complex interactions. In everyday conversation we engage in this kind of exchange without having to dissect what was said. We may look back wondering just where the digressions began, what triggered off a certain thread in the conversation. In an interview it is not enough simply to let it go where it will; to become aware of the interview's direction and to guide it where you want it to go needs an alert and analytic approach.

SUMMARY

In this chapter we showed the effects of different sequences of question and response upon the interview as a whole. We moved from the simplest structure of single, unlinked question-response combinations, to chain structures and complex interactive structures with feedback loops. Examining these structural patterns is a valuable tool for checking on the way an interview has proceeded, and reveals sources of bias and problems in probing and remembering in complex interactions.

In the next chapter we will show how to develop your skills further, paying particular attention to how you interpret the responses.

ACTIVITIES FOR STUDENTS

For practice, first tape-record five minutes of a casual conversation, then construct some questions on the same topic and try these out as if in an interview. Perhaps a fellow student will be willing to act as respondent.

What structures emerged from each of these? How did they differ from each other? Construct the configuration which best represents what took place in your interview segment.

In your five minutes, what was taken up with the opening phase, the main body of the questions and the closing phase?

Now check to see how many of the questions set out in the earlier part of this chapter were answered.

chapter

6

INTERPRETING THE RESPONSES

Because of the dynamic nature of the interviewer–respondent relationship, the interviewer needs to be constantly interpreting and evaluating the meaning of the replies to the questions. The words people use do not always express overtly what their real feelings are, and in trying to respond to difficult questions many people experience problems in finding precise words to explain what they are feeling or thinking. In responding to questions which are conceptually demanding, many will have difficulty in giving an adequate answer. They may fumble for words, mumble, speak too fast or too slow, take long pauses, resort to catch-phrases, and repeat themselves.

How is the interviewer to interpret what the respondent is saying? Does the answer represent the respondent's true opinion or attitude, or is the respondent trying to avoid giving the true answer? Is the response consistent with what was said in reply to an earlier question? These are questions which have to be dealt with in interpreting the meaning of the responses. They have to be addressed as the interview proceeds. In this chapter we will show some ways of handling these problems.

THE RESPONDENT'S BEHAVIOUR

It would be very simple for interpreting the responses if all respondents replied willingly, truthfully and in carefully phrased terms to the questions they are asked. In practice, however, the interviewer is likely to find a much more complex situation. Below are some of the most common ways in which respondents react to interviewers' questions.

Inconsistency

The response to a later question may contradict an earlier response. The interviewer's problem is to establish which is correct. Was it deliberate? If so, why was the second answer different? Or did what took place in the course of the interview help to reach a truer answer? If so, perhaps the intervening questions helped the respondent to think more clearly or perhaps to feel more comfortable with the interview situation.

Non-cooperation

To what extent is the respondent giving cooperation? Is it being given willingly or grudgingly? Is there coercion in the respondent's compliance? There are many situations in which the respondent may give only superficial compliance. The interviewer needs to be able to identify the degree of cooperation not only because of the need to obtain truthful answers but also because of its effect on the interviewer–respondent relationship.

Evasion

In this case the respondent avoids the thrust of the question by talking around it but never actually answering it. Other ways of evading are the straightforward refusal to answer—for example, 'No comment', 'I can't answer that', 'I can't remember'. Hesitating before responding may accompany the evasion. Yet another way of evading the response is to bluster, in an attempt to turn the focus towards the interviewer away from the respondent. This is the not-uncommon defence of the hostile respondent.

Inaccuracy in recall

In this situation the respondent is not uncooperative but has difficulty in remembering clearly. Possible reasons need to be considered. For example, there may be a blockage because of some stressful associations. It may be that the respondent has a great need to appear in a favourable light, or the actual circumstance has been given a more socially acceptable interpretation, which remains as the person's accepted belief. Of course, the person genuinely may have simply forgotten.

Lack of verbal skills

Many respondents may have difficulty in expressing themselves clearly and precisely because they lack the verbal skills to do so. Several factors may contribute to this difficulty. They may not be accustomed to using verbal means to express themselves but more usually resort to actions; they may be more used to a different language style such as frequent use of colloquial language and slang; they may lack the vocabulary to say what they mean. These respondents may spend a long time trying to express themselves in words, with many pauses and fumbles.

Conceptual difficulty

This problem is concerned with the ability to understand the questions and their implications rather than with the respondent's ability to express attitudes or opinions in precise verbal terms. The topic itself may be quite a difficult one, requiring a complex response which is difficult to think through. However, individual differences in conceptual abilities will affect the comprehension of questions and the quality of responses at any level of item difficulty.

Emotional state

The emotional state of the respondent at the time of the interview can have a marked effect on the relationship between interviewer and respondent and on the quality of the responses. Anxiety, depression, nervous apprehension, lack of self-esteem and concern about one's lack of ability tend to have negative effects; as do exaggerated euphoria and abnormally high levels of self-evaluation, which occur as a result of taking part in the interview. These respondents may have difficulty in concentrating on the question and organising their thoughts in responding. They may prefer non-verbal ways of expressing emotion to verbal means.

Bias

Many of these kinds of reactions by respondents produce some kinds of bias in their answers. The self-serving bias of the distortion which seeks to portray the speaker in a favourable light is not uncommon. Bias could occur in the interpretation of the question as well as in the answer. It can be a conscious prejudice or an underlying attitude so ingrained as to be part of their whole way of thinking.

AN INTERVIEWER'S INTERPRETATIVE SKILLS

All of these behaviours present in the respondent's replies can affect the interviewer's interpretation of their meaning. The interviewer's task is to interpret the response as accurately as possible. This involves many interrelated skills, including the skills of listening, speaking, understanding and remembering, being aware of the developing structure, skills of probing and taking account of the non-verbal messages which may support or deny the words that are spoken.

Listening skills

For the interviewer, listening must be an active attempt to interpret what the speaker is intending to convey. In everyday conversation people do not pay attention to grammatical forms. They do not speak in carefully constructed sentences but convey their meanings in many different ways. The listener must make use of more than the surface meaning to interpret the speaker's intentions. At the beginning of the interview the interviewer will need to listen carefully to the respondent to be alert to these language styles for, as the interview develops and the respondent becomes more involved, they may become more pronounced. The interviewer must pay attention not only to what is being said but to how it is being said.

Hearing is not the same as listening, but it is a necessary condition. The interviewer should check at the beginning that both interviewer and respondent are in a position to hear each other. Constant interruptions are to be avoided; the respondent will be annoyed at being constantly asked to repeat what was said but will also be likely to interpret the request to repeat as indicating an unacceptable reply. Any recording equipment used should be tried out first to ensure that both questions and responses can be heard.

Speaking skills

While interviewers must expect a whole range of speaking skills in the respondent, much can be done in their own speech styles to ensure that the questions have been both heard and understood.

Speed of delivery is important: neither too fast nor too slow. Volume should be not too loud, but loud enough to be heard throughout the whole of the question. Do not trail off, or drop the voice at the end of the sentence, especially at the end of a question. A voice pitched low is easier to listen to. Voices tend to rise when the speaker is anxious or excited. A calm, clear enunciation is most effective, but there is no need to adopt enunciation which is not natural. Choose language which is able to be understood by the respondent.

Conceptual skills

If good interviewing demands active listening, it demands active thinking to an even greater degree as the interviewer strives to understand the meaning of the responses. How the respondent reacts during the interview has to be considered and the questioning adapted according to the interviewer's interpretation of the respondent's behaviour.

Remembering

As the interview proceeds, the demand on the interviewer to remember what was said earlier increases. Unless the structure is of the simplest type, in which there is no direct connection between questions, what was said in reply to an earlier question may affect not only the response to a later question but also the way in which later questions are phrased.

Awareness of the developing structure

Remembering what has been taking place is essential to being aware of how the structure of the interview is developing. The complex structures with feedback which arise from probing (such as figures 5.4 and 5.5 in chapter 5) rely to a great degree on the interviewer being able to remember and make use of earlier responses. If the interviewer loses track of the direction the interview is taking, it can very easily fall into the kind of sequential structure with channelling described in chapter 5.

Patience

It is not only in clinical interviewing and counselling that the interviewer needs to develop patience. When the respondent hesitates or fumbles with attempts to express ideas, the unskilled interviewer might try to elicit a quicker response by interrupting with words such as 'I think I know what you mean', or 'I think I understand what you are trying to say'. This is a very risky practice as the interviewer might be quite wrong. An impatient interviewer might, while the respondent pauses to think, try again to ask the same question with 'let me ask you that again' or 'let me put that a different way'. It can be difficult to wait, but intervening before the respondent is ready to reply can disrupt the flow of thoughts and have a negative effect upon the relationship. Better ways of handling this situation are shown in the section below on probing.

Patience is particularly relevant in interviews with children, the aged, anxious respondents and people with disabilities (which are treated later: see chapters 9, 11, 12). The interviewer must pace the questioning to suit the pace of the respondent.

PROBING

Probing has many functions in interpreting responses. It can be used to clarify meaning, to extend the range and quality of replies, to examine consistency, to give encouragement and to reduce anxiety.

As probe questions have the function of obtaining a more complete or more accurate statement of the respondent's ideas, it is important that they be expressed in terms which encourage the respondent to organise their thoughts. They need to be supportive but without showing bias.

Gorden (1969) identified seven types of probing: the silent probe, encouragement, immediate clarification, retrospective clarification, immediate elaboration, retrospective elaboration and mutation.

The silent probe

The silent probe uses non-verbal means of conveying that the interviewer is asking for more information. It may be a nod of the head to offer encouragement, or a raised eyebrow to indicate a further query or surprise. This type of probe requires mutual understanding of its meaning to be effective.

A very useful type of silent probe is the pause. Simply waiting for the respondent to continue instead of proceeding to another question can indicate that more information is wanted. The pause can help respondents to collect their thoughts, and to review their answer thus far.

Encouragement

Encouragement can be given non-verbally, with minimal language or by longer expressions of empathy and understanding. Minimal verbal expressions such as 'Uh huh', 'Mm', and simple phrases such as 'I see', and 'Go on' can give encouragement. One problem here is how to avoid making an evaluative judgement which suggests that the respondent's reply is incorrect or in some way unacceptable.

Immediate clarification

Clarification asks for more information to explain an answer more clearly. Immediate clarification refers to the response just given to the last question. There are many ways of asking for clarification. For example, 'I'm not sure that I got that exactly. Could you explain a little more fully?' or 'Can you explain that to me again?'

Retrospective clarification

In retrospective clarification the interviewer goes back to an earlier response. For example, 'Previously you said ... Could you explain that to me a little more fully now in the light of what you have just told me?'

Immediate elaboration

Immediate elaboration goes beyond the immediate response to explore it in greater depth. The interviewer might ask for reasons, or for any other aspects to the given response. This type of probe can become very complex, invoking the complex structures with feedback loops described in chapter 5.

Retrospective elaboration

Retrospective elaboration is similar to immediate elaboration in going beyond the response but differs from it in that the interviewer and respondent return to earlier questions and responses. The typical structure is that shown in figure 5.5 (chapter 5).

The interviewer may also use retrospective elaboration to review progress so far and to check on whether major points have been covered adequately. This has the function of giving feedback to the respondent.

Mutation

Mutation is the term used by Gorden to refer to the use of the next question to shift to another topic. Such questions produce the linkages between the groups of questions in the constellated structures of figure 5.6 (chapter 5).

THE NON-VERBAL MESSAGES

Although interviews are based upon the use of words as the major medium of communication, at the same time non-verbal behaviour is conveying messages between interviewer and respondent. The non-verbal messages are the medium of feelings and emotions, and it is claimed (Argyle, 1992; Gallois & Callan, 1997) that these responses are produced more automatically than words. They are multi-channelled, involving body, face and voice, and all may be activated at the same time. They may also occur at the same time as the verbal exchange. It follows that both interviewer and respondent are sending out non-verbal messages to each other in the course of an interview. It is also likely that the non-verbal message will at times contradict the verbal message.

Channels involving the body include general appearance, body posture, gestures, movement, touch, distance and orientation.

General appearance

Clothes, hairstyle, cleanliness, and deportment lead to instant impressions, and to stereotyping into categories. Neat and tidy or scruffy and dishevelled, frumpish or fashionable, young or old—what is the first impression of this person's occupation, social status, or intelligence? Appearance is always considered by selection interviewing panels and job applicants are often taught how to appear to their best advantage when going for an interview (especially in today's situation of high unemployment). Many other types of interview can also be influenced by appearances: for example, over-the-counter information seeking, interviews with bank managers, with solicitors and the police. The influence is likely to be greatest when this is the first occasion the interviewer and respondent meet.

Body posture

When we are attending closely to what a person is saying, we tend to lean forward towards that person, but that is not the only interpretation of a forward-leaning posture. An aggressive, angry attitude can also be expressed with a forward posture, the difference being revealed in facial expression, a clenched fist or general tenseness. Individual differences in these responses also occur. Anger and aggression may be expressed less openly by a rigid erect posture. A friendly attitude is indicated by a more relaxed posture with head and shoulders in a relaxed forward position and hands open.

Kafer (1993, p72) stresses that inferences should be made in the context of what is occurring at the time: 'Slouching with arms and legs splayed out could be interpreted as either a "don't care" attitude or one of relaxation and ease. In the same way sitting upright with shoulders back could be an indication of attentiveness and readiness to participate or a defensive pose.' Some people who are actually very unsure of themselves may adopt a posture which is meant to suggest ease and relaxation, but if the situation is in fact threatening—for example, a teenager being questioned by police—the posture may be interpreted as antagonistic because of its inappropriateness. Social and cultural differences abound.

Gestures

Gestures may accompany verbal responses (and questions) or can serve instead of words. When accompanying words, gestures can serve to emphasise, to add extra information and to express emotions. They can indicate boredom or lack of interest. They can also be used to hide or de-emphasise what the words imply. Hence, they can be indicators of conflicting messages.

Individual differences in styles of self-expression show differences in the style and frequency of using gestures. Cultural differences in the use of gesture are well-known: compare, for example, French or Italian with Japanese conversational styles. Social backgrounds and social contexts within a culture also vary as to how much use of gesture is acceptable in normal conversation. Hence, where expansive gesturing is frowned upon, covert gestures can appear when a person is under stress.

The use of gesture increases with excitement and with nervousness. Excitement tends to be associated with more expansive gestures, with larger body movements, arms waving and hands open and outspread. Signs of nervousness are revealed in increases in small movements, especially hand movements, in touching the face, hand- or foot-tapping and, by girls, twisting their long hair into coils. Shaking a leg under the table out of sight is a frequent indicator of stress in those cultures which discourage outward expressions of emotion. Twisting a hankerchief or tearing a tissue into shreds is another sign. People do wring their hands in situations of extreme anguish.

Gestures for reinforcement and confirmation with or without language include nodding in affirmation and shaking the head. Shaking the head can express disagreement but can also indicate surprise, as in 'That's amazing!'.

Movement

Getting up suddenly in the middle of an interview, pacing up and down, and leaving the room suddenly all indicate an emotional response. Although more extreme in action than gestures, this behaviour may not indicate greater degrees of anxiety. Individual differences have to be taken into account.

Distance

The distance between two people has both physical and psychological qualities. How far distant does one need to be to feel comfortable with another person? Physical closeness indicates intimacy and to preserve social distance an interviewer and respondent will choose a position which is not too close.

Touching the respondent is to be avoided. Touching can show intimacy but it can also show aggression. For example, an angry respondent might lean forward to grab at the interview's arm or clothing.

In interviews in which both interviewer and respondent are seated in a room, the respondent's physical distance from the interviewer is fixed initially by the arrangement of the furniture. To show resistance the respondent may resort to increasing the psychological distance by straightening her or his back, by sitting up straight in the chair, or leaning further back.

In interviews in public places such as in the street or a shopping centre, the distance is also affected by noise factors and the number of people nearby.

How close is too close? This can be tried out by invading someone's personal space. Begin by standing a comfortable distance away, then move steadily closer. At some point you will see a change in the person—a slight backward movement, looking away or down to avoid eye contact, until finally they move away. (For research and examples, see Sommer, 1969; Proshansky, Ittelson & Rivlin, 1976.)

Facial expressions

Much research has been carried out on how people interpret facial expressions. Most studies (Eckman, 1982; Eckman & Friesen, 1975) have confirmed that the emotions of happiness, surprise, sadness and anger are generally recognisable from facial expressions. The table of facial signals of emotional states (from Kafer, 1993, p.72) sets out the facial expressions associated with emotions.

Facial signals of emotional states

Emotional state	Facial signal
Anger	Eyes wide open, eyebrows lowered, mouth muscles tense
Surprise	Eyes wide open, eyebrows raised, mouth open and relaxed
Happiness	Eyes screwed up, eyebrows neutral, mouth elongated with corners up
Sadness	Eyes lowered, eyebrows down, mouth corners down
Boredom	Eyes and eyebrows neutral, mouth turned down
Fear	Eyes wide open, eyebrows raised, mouth open with corners drawn back
Self-satisfaction	Eyes closed up, eyebrows neutral, corners of the mouth up

Eye contact

It can be seen from the table of facial signals how much we make use of the eyes when making inferences about emotional states on the basis of facial expressions. Eye contact enables a person to gain that information quickly. Hence, in interviewing, eye contact between interviewer and respondent gives information about the relationship, about the respondent's emotional state and helps to gain and maintain the respondent's attention.

In Australian culture looking directly at a person we are addressing or who is speaking to us is seen as showing attention, and being polite. Avoiding direct eye contact is seen as furtive, inattentive, bored, nervous, and even fearful. However, not all cultures regard direct eye contact as polite or showing attention. Aboriginal Australians tend to sit side by side, as do American Indians, while children in many cultures are not encouraged to look directly at adults (see also chapters 9 and 13).

Even where direct eye contact is acceptable or encouraged, to gaze directly too long is seen as impolite, confronting and intrusive. Try this out for yourself by taking a seat opposite a person who is not familiar to you. Try to make eye contact, then look steadily at that person's face. How long before that person will look away, how long before he or she gets up and leaves? (But only try this out in a comfortable environment, with fellow students, or you might receive a much more abusive response!)

Smiling

Smiling is usually seen as accepting and offering acceptance of the other, indicating the presence of a good relationship or the intention to develop such a relationship. Nevertheless, subtle variations in the smiling face can convey contrary emotional states. The superficial forced smile, the sexual leer, the smirk of self-satisfaction and the smile of dominance are well-known.

Voice

The non-verbal aspects of voice usually refer to the tone of voice, and include such qualities as pitch, breathiness, volume and rising and falling inflexion. Together, these voice qualities can convey various meanings to the same words. For example, compare the following variations.

- 'You didn't do it, did you?'—The question suggests the answer 'No' is expected.
- 'You [with the emphasis on 'You'] didn't do it, did you?'—The implication is that someone else did it.
- 'You didn't do it, did you.'—This is said as a statement which affirms that the person in question did not do it.
- 'You didn't [with the emphasis on 'didn't'] do it, did you?'—Here the speaker is expressing incredulous surprise. The emphasis suggests that the person was not expected to do it.

Try out as many variations on phrases similar to the above example as you can.

The emotions expressed by the tone of voice that are of particular importance in interviewing are those that serve as signs of stress and anxiety in the respondent and those that denote calmness on the part of the interviewer. It is also important to keep individual differences in mind; pitch may be associated with the quality of the person's normal voice, children and females tending to have higher voices than males. It is the change in tone of voice which should alert the interviewer to an emotional response.

Interpreting conflicting non-verbal and verbal messages

If the non-verbal messages are produced more automatically than the verbal responses, we must expect that there should be less control over this behaviour than over what is said. Hence, we can expect that often the respondent will send out conflicting messages, in which the body, the face or the tone of voice conveys a message at odds with the verbal response.

The interviewer's task is to find what is the actual meaning and the reason for the difference. Is it a deliberate attempt to obscure the underlying emotion or lie about the behaviour being asked about? Is the respondent being socially acquiescent and avoiding a response which might offend? Or is the respondent merely confused?

The way to find out is through probing for clarification and elaboration. Beware of being confrontational. Aggressive interviewing will elicit defensive responses, which reinforce the original statement. Remember, too, that both interviewer and respondent send out non-verbal messages. Whatever means the respondent uses, the interviewer needs to maintain a calm presenting manner. Controlling facial expressions and gestures which exhibit disbelief, anger or disapproval is essential to retain trust. Smiling must reflect a genuine interest and accepting attitude. Genuine attempts to understand, and to develop empathy will usually meet with an accepting response.

SUMMARY

This chapter has brought you to a stage where you can now draw together the various strands which go to make up the dynamic totality of an interview. We have now covered the setting up of the interview, the development of the interviewer–respondent relationship, the wording of the questions, following the structural development of the interview, moving backward and forward with probing, interpreting both the verbal responses and the non-verbal messages. In the course of practising your techniques, you will find as your skills develop that interviewing is an absorbing and fascinating pursuit. In the following chapters we show how to apply these skills in a variety of situations.

ACTIVITIES FOR STUDENTS

Practice in pairs, wherever possible using video recording, each taking a turn as interviewer and respondent.

In your role as interviewer, make up a short set of questions on a topic which will be demanding conceptually and likely to arouse an emotional response.

In your role as respondent, answer the questions in whatever way you think appropriate but do not offer an answer which gives your complete views on the subject. Let the interviewer try to find out.

As the interviewer, use probing to elicit the respondent's views.

Record both questions and responses.

Play back. Examine your interview in terms of: clarity of the questions; presence of bias; correct interpretation of the responses; effectiveness of probing; interpretation of the non-verbal cues; rapport; structural direction.

chapter

7

INTERVIEWING IN RESEARCH

Many of the types of interview described in chapter 2 are used in research. In this chapter we will concentrate on research which is designed to use interviewing as the principal method of data collection rather than as an adjunct to laboratory experiments.

When would one choose to use interviewing over other research methods? Experimentalists who use laboratory controlled tasks often regard their methods as more 'scientific'; others regard test performance and responses to questionnaires as more 'objective'. It is proposed here that interviewing will be more efficient in the following situations.

- If you want to know what people are thinking.
- If you want to explore the reasons and motivations for the attitudes and opinions of people.
- If you are not satisfied with the low response rate that can so often occur with a questionnaire.
- If the topic is threatening.
- If ideas are likely to be difficult to express.

- If your subjects have difficulty in communicating.
- If your subjects are likely to be hostile to other methods.
- If your subjects are in trouble, are anti-social or out of the mainstream of society.

Can interviewing be as objective as other methods of data gathering? Other methods are never completely free of the subjectivity which is involved in the relationship between researcher and subject. As was pointed out in chapter 1, the experimental researcher also has to make personal contact with subjects to establish a relationship of acquiescence and cooperation, and at the conclusion of the experimental session has to debrief the subject satisfactorily.

Problems of post-hoc analysis of old data

Many of the interview types described in chapter 2 are not planned for producing research data. Nevertheless, such interviews may later be drawn upon to provide research evidence, but there are many problems inherent in this practice. Different times, different purposes, and different contexts, together with different subject and sample characteristics—all these factors produce many variables which cannot be controlled or accounted for over the whole group of interviews which provide the data base.

A further question relates to the consistency in the records taken. The interviews may have been carried out by different interviewers, whose methods of recording may have varied substantially. Policies in large organisations change from time to time. The clinician, counsellor or social worker who wants to trace some development over a period of time will be familiar with the difficulty of obtaining the degree of consistency in the records which is necessary to track down the evidence needed. At times this kind of evaluation after the event has to be done. Here, however, we will deal only with research which is designed with the use of interviewing as the immediate data source rather than in a post-hoc evaluation.

The theoretical basis

As in all research, we begin by examining the problem in the light of existing theoretical explanations and the research evidence from previous work in that field. This preliminary work elicits the specific aspects which need to be investigated further. From this point we can then express our aims more precisely and formulate hypotheses in formal terms. The questions which will constitute the main body of the interview will arise directly from this first step.

Sampling

This first theoretical analysis will also lead to setting up the criteria to be used in deciding upon the characteristics of the sample of subjects to be interviewed.

Background information will need to be ascertained to be able to describe the sample finally obtained. This sort of information generally includes variables such as age, gender, socio-economic status and geographic location. Other relevant background variables might include those more closely related to the specific issue: such as marital status and other persons resident in the home, in the case of a study of family relations; or performance in school examinations, in a study on high school students' attitudes to schooling.

The question of how the sample is to be obtained has to be considered. Ethical questions of confidentiality have to be resolved and, if other organisations are to be involved, permission to interview may have to be obtained.

Sampling for research using interviewing must be as carefully controlled as in any other research involving humans. The actual target number will depend on the frequency of the behaviour to be investigated and the availability of subjects. Unrealistic expectations (such as a stratified random sample of the whole population) may have to be curbed if the project is a modest one to be carried out by a single researcher or small group. Student researchers seldom have such a luxury as the large team needed for a population-wide study. In such restricted conditions it is all the more important to establish workable criteria highlighting the important variables and stick to them.

The research design

As with other methods, the research design has to be set up so that the variables under consideration can be isolated.

When the interview is the sole source of data, the content of the questions has to embody the research design. An 'experimental' group can be contrasted with a 'control' group, or two or more groups which differ on a variable such as age or gender can be compared. There could be only one item for each variable or each variable could be composed of several items, the group of items contributing to a composite measure. The way these measures can be obtained is treated below in the section on coding. Frequencies or scores can be used according to the nature of the data.

In another design the interview questions are supplementary to another data source. The interview questions may refer to performance on a task, as in Piagetian testing or in studies of children's social development after the style of Selman (1980), where the questions are linked directly to a child's performance and reasoning. There are many techniques used in counselling and work with children which take this approach. This design produces a set of related data for each of the control and comparison groups, for each question. Responses and reasons can be treated separately or combined to form a total score. Note that these can be scores rather than frequencies. Criteria for scoring need to be set up according to whatever theoretical basis is being used.

Another design is to relate responses to the interview questions to performance on another measure, such as an attitude scale, which elicits different, but possibly related, ideas or attitudes. Examination of such a relationship may be exploratory, or may test a relationship predicted by a hypothesis. The appropriateness of this type of design depends on how compatible the two sets of data are—for example, if the scale values are in scores while the interview data are in frequencies.

Preparing the interview schedule

For research the interview schedule must be able to be used consistently with the same meaning with all the respondents in the samples, yet at the same time allow for individual differences in response styles. In practice, this means that the core set of questions has to remain constant while probing can explore reasons and account for individual differences in language, conceptualisation and readiness to respond.

Before the data collection can begin, a number of questions have to be answered.

- Will the questions mean the same to all respondents?
- Is the vocabulary appropriate?
- Will the phrasing be easily understood?
- How long will it take to administer the schedule?
- Is there any bias in the content or in the way the questions are phrased?
- What is the best way to introduce the topic?
- Is all the information best obtained by asking or should other sources be used?
- What method will be used to record the answers?

Preparing the response sheets

As was shown in chapter 4, many kinds of question format can be used, each with its own characteristic method of obtaining answers. As the questions are constructed you need also to prepare the associated response sheets. These should be prepared at the same time as the set of questions, not simply tacked on afterwards.

Pilot studies

A pilot study should always be carried out before the major data collection begins. Pilot studies can include qualitative examinations of the questions, and a small sample of respondents can be interviewed using what is intended to be the form of the interview schedule. Check that all the points raised above in the section on 'Preparing the interview schedule' have been answered satisfactorily. Reliability and validity checks should be carried out to show how the items are behaving. The pilot studies also provide early feedback for the interviewers. More than one pilot study may be needed before the final version is achieved.

Reliability

Reliability in relation to interviewing as a research method refers to the degree of consistency that the interview has for the person or persons interviewed. Reliability could be shown in two ways, either by repeating the interview on a later occasion to find whether the same responses would be obtained or by examining the extent to which the same questions given in a different form within the same interview would elicit the same responses. In deciding whether the response is the same, we consider the content rather than the actual words used. Hence, the topic could be addressed in several different question formats: for example, answers to an open-ended question could be compared with the answer to a multiple-choice or rank-order question on the same topic.

Cronbach's Alpha is a statistical measure used for testing reliability in the sense of internal consistency. Another method used commonly in psychological testing is that of splitting the total number of items into two by random allocation or by alternate items and correlating the halves with each other. The Spearman-Brown correction formula is then used to measure reliability. See Anastasi & Urbina (1997) for a full discussion of Cronbach's Alpha and split-half methods. In many interviews the split-half method may not be practical because of the dynamic development within an interview which makes such equivalence unlikely to occur.

An aspect of reliability which is of critical importance in research interviewing is the reliability of the interviewer or interviewers. When the one interviewer has to collect the data from a number of respondents and when more than one interviewer is employed, the question arises as to how consistently they carry out the task. Does the single interviewer keep to the planned schedule of questions, and does the team of interviewers follow the instructions precisely or do they vary their approaches to such an extent that the variations introduced make comparability dubious. Use of multi methods of recording, including audiotaping and videotaping, together with pilot studies and training will help to improve reliability.

Validity

Validity is concerned with how well the research instrument measures what it is intended to measure. In interviewing research this question relates to how confident one can be that the content of the interview is actually doing its intended job. Hence, we need to consider validity in the context of purpose to be served.

Construct validity refers to how well the measures reflect the underlying constructs, or theoretical basis. It is the most inclusive term, and in the case of interview data refers to how closely the questioning is linked to the constructs which are being researched. Validating against other criteria which are known to measure the construct is a frequent strategy.

Content validity is about whether the questions sample the field of behaviour adequately.

Face validity is what the questions are seen to be about in the perception of the respondent. If the respondent cannot see the point of the questions from the way in which they have been introduced, the interview will not be seen as having face validity by that respondent. This could occur if the interviewer has presented the purpose of the interview in a way which is more favourable than it actually is. For example, a research interview whose true purpose is to probe risk-taking behaviour and drug abuse might be presented simply as a survey on people's lifestyles. The reaction of respondents who find that they have been misled is likely to be hostile.

Predictive validity refers to the efficiency with which the responses in the interview will predict future performance on the relevant behaviour. It may be that the interview is being used to select for a position (see chapter 8), or for allocating clients to a treatment or rehabilitation program. The predictive validity would be the degree to which the selection or allocation predicted the later performance in the field. One problem is that knowledge of the interview responses and the value judgements made about the interviewee might influence later evaluation.

For a thorough treatment of both reliability and validity, see Anastasi & Urbina (1997).

Training of interviewers

If the research program involves using a number of interviewers, a training program needs to be set up to ensure that all interviewers use the interview schedule, recording equipment and response sheets effectively. Aspects of technique can be developed, problems encountered in pilot work discussed and resolved, and methods of recording responses worked over until a satisfactory skill level is attained. Feedback can be given, individually or as a group, with video- or tape-recorder. Formal statistical checks on reliability should be carried out.

If only one interviewer is to carry out the research (as may well be the case for a student project or thesis), time should be allowed for developing one's skills and checking on reliability before embarking on the main data collection. Do not rely solely on your own evaluation but ask another person to respond to the questions posed above. Do a small number of interviews, about one-tenth of the total required, as a pilot study. Use a tape-recorder to gain feedback.

Coding

As the data are obtained they need to be entered into the computer ready for analysis. This stage involves coding the responses into categories and allocating each response with its code value.

With closed format questions such as multiple-choice and rank-order items the categories are pre-set in the question. However, should an extra category be added—by asking if the respondent wished to add any other answer not included in the given set—these responses have to be categorised on the basis of the type of responses obtained. If there are very few of these a simple 'other' category may be sufficient, to be explained later in relation to the other replies by that sample of respondents. If there is a large number of these it will suggest that the question did not cover the relevant aspects very well. This should be picked up and corrected in the pilot work.

With open-ended questions the researcher has to set up the coding system from two points of departure: the theoretical range and the actual range of responses.

The theoretical range includes all possible types of answer. The content could include either scale positions on one or more dimensions or categories of responses based on the literature review and hypotheses, with the possibility of an 'other' category if needed.

If a single dimension is expected, the responses can be coded into positions ranging from extremely low to extremely high. Locating responses along this dimension would require definitions of what each position represented. A simple four-point scale often provides sufficient discrimination for practical purposes. A four-point scale avoids the midpoint, which is open to many abuses, such as using it for evasive answers which avoid a decisive response. With probing, the interviewer can usually find the side on which the answer fits most comfortably and whether the respondent is avoiding an answer or truly cannot decide.

The same criteria apply to responses which are theoretically expected to fall on more than one dimension.

Although theoretically the response categories must cover all possible types of response, in practice the actual range of responses obtained may be relatively small. These responses may not fit along a single dimension but fall into distinct categories To code them for the analysis, it is essential that the categories be independent of one another. Where it appears impossible to separate more than one aspect of such responses a combined response type can be allocated to a category of its own. These categories can be grouped later according to their frequency, combining them in such a was as to make rational groupings, not merely grouping them on the basis of the small numbers in the cell. For example, an open-ended question on marital status might yield the following variants:

Single, never married, no children or any number of children
Single, in de facto relationship, no children or any number of children
Single, divorced, no children or as above
Married, no children
Married, children as above

Preparation for the analysis

Wherever possible the responses should be entered into the computer as the data collection is proceeding. This means that the coding system must be flexible enough to allow for those unanticipated responses in the 'other' categories. It is easier to combine categories than to create new categories later.

The statistical treatment will depend on the research design and the nature of the data, whether in scores, frequencies or rank orders.

Because of the great variety of responses that interviewing can uncover, and the wealth of information it can reveal in regard to the motivations, reasoning and antecedent conditions contributing to the answers, it is not unlikely that the researcher will have more information than can be analysed easily (especially if only one student researcher has to do it all). Care will therefore be needed to select the data most relevant to the research question posed.

QUALITATIVE ANALYSIS

One of the great advantages of using interviews is that many and varied methods can be used to obtain and analyse the data. In this section some qualitative approaches are described.

Case studies

Qualitative analysis of selected case studies may be a valuable adjunct to the statistical treatment. Such case studies provide in-depth reports from the respondent's personal viewpoint. They put flesh on the bones of the statistics, bringing together the discrete components of the analysis into an integrated whole. They are also able to deal with individual cases which do not fit easily into the broad picture derived from the statistical analysis.

Content analysis

Content analysis considers the nature of the verbal communication. The level of analysis can be directed to words, phrases or themes. Responses to the interview questions are transcribed into textual form and then categorised according to the unit of measurement selected. This method has been described by King (1994) as quasi-statistical, in that statistical analyses can be carried out comparing individuals or groups on their distribution across categories. Computer programs for content analysis are now available and computerised content analysis has been found (Morris, 1994) to be as reliable as human-coded analyses. Proponents of computerised analysis (Fielding & Lee, 1991; Tesch, 1991) argue strongly for its efficiency.

Discourse analysis

This multidisciplinary approach (Potter & Wetherall, 1987; Lupton, 1992) is concerned with the critical analysis of meaning within its socio-cultural and political context. The interview is treated in two dimensions: textual and contextual. Discourse analysis is directed towards the interpretation of themes rather than the frequency of words, phrases or themes as in content analysis. Much depends upon the subjective organisation of the interview material by the researcher. Lupton (p.149) says:

> Proponents of discourse analysis make no claims as to the objectivity or universal truth of their insights ... Discourse theory openly acknowledges the inevitability of a theory being context and observer specific; indeed the role of discourse analysis as a critical tool requires that the commentator's particular perspective be made explicit.

Validation is by extensive use of actual textual material and comparing other interpretations of the same material. In the case of interviews, detailed transcriptions of the texts are used. Interviews may be carried out over several occasions before the final interpretation is made.

Multi method approaches

Multi method research is the application of two or more different methods to the one research problem. Leonard (1995) argues that, although it has many advocates, multi method research has not been used frequently, partly because of the extra work involved but, more seriously, because of the conceptual problem of dealing with any discrepancies which are revealed in the different sets of analysis. The terms 'cross-validation' and 'triangulation' are used to refer to comparisons between two or more approaches to the same problem. With these methods each approach is regarded as providing its own perspective on the issue. For example, in Leonard's study in the field of children's social development, a quasi-experimental study using puppets as stimulus figures was given to the children, while in a companion home study the mothers were trained in observational techniques. With the many ways in which interviews can be conducted, multi media methods could combine quantitative and qualitative approaches very effectively.

USE OF INTERVIEWING IN CROSS-CULTURAL RESEARCH

Cross-cultural research requires a number of conditions to be met which do not arise when working within a single culture. Individual and within-culture group differences still have to be considered, but the main focus is on the influence of cultural factors on the behaviour under study. To make any valid inferences about the role of these factors we have to take great care in setting up the research plan and collecting the data.

Cross-cultural studies are of three main kinds. One is looking for a universal explanation of some aspect of behaviour, for example to find whether some trait, relationship or developmental trend occurs in a similar way or has a similar function in a wide variety of cultural contexts. A second concentrates on bringing out the culturally specific aspects, contrasting two or more cultural groups. The third is concerned with the interaction of people from differing cultural backgrounds. Interviewing is used in all three.

Cross-cultural studies can be carried out within a multicultural country (such as Australia) or in cooperation with co-workers in another country of differing cultural background. More extensive research programs can involve cooperation in a large number of countries.

Before we go further, it will be useful to clarify the difference between a cross-cultural study and a cross-national study. Cross-national refers to comparisons based on national differences. A good example is the International Educational Achievement Studies, which compare the performance of schoolchildren from a wide range of countries on standardised tests in mathematics, science and other school subjects. In a cross-national study involving Australia and Malaysia, for example, the many ethnic and cultural groups within each country might not be identified in the samples. A cross-cultural study would be more interested in the similarities and differences among the ethnic and cultural groups and how these were influenced by factors based in their cultural values and traditional practices. The sampling would select in such a way as to identify each of the cultural or ethnic groups separately both within and across the two countries. The analysis would be carried out with the data from each cultural group compared on the variables studied.

The theoretical issues of the definitions of culture and ethnicity need not concern us greatly here. Much has been written elsewhere on this question (see, for example, Thomas, 1986; Segall, Dasen, Berry & Poortinga, 1990; Keats, 1997). The methodological issues which are of interest here are the same whether we are working with samples defined by culture or by ethnic identity. Issues relating to comparability include the functional equivalence of concepts, the language or languages used in the interviews, problems of sampling, motivation and familiarity with the tasks and responding to questions. When working with a team, the selection and training of the interviewers becomes very important, especially if the interviewers have to use interpreters (see chapter 13).

Comparability of the concepts

The first necessity is for functional equivalence of the topic to be studied: that is, it should have the same meaning in each of the cultures involved. The interviewer will not make much progress if the concepts implicit in the themes in the interview are so foreign to the respondent's experience that the respondent simply does not know what the interviewer is talking about. It is necessary to explore these ideas at the beginning to ensure that there is a common understanding of the topic.

This problem is best resolved when researchers from each of the cultures involved work together as a team to plan the project. The research topic will be most acceptable if it is one of mutual interest and meets a need felt by each of the cultural groups involved. It should not be a case of one researcher imposing his or her problem upon another in a different culture merely for that researcher's own benefit.

Language and translation

Two aspects need to be considered: the language used in the interview schedule and the language used by the interviewers. To construct the schedule you have to begin somewhere, and that will usually be with the language of the chief researcher or a language common to all members of the team. Today, English is so widespread that it may be the choice to begin with.

The research interview should be conducted in the respondent's preferred language. This is generally the native language; however, if the respondent prefers to use a second language such as English, but is not proficient in that language, a written version should also be made available.

When the schedule has to be translated into the other languages to be employed, how can you be confident that the translated version will have the same function as the original? The method favoured by most cross-cultural researchers is that of back translation (Brislin, 1986). With this method the first translation is then translated back into the original language by another translator and the two versions are compared. This process is repeated until problems are resolved.

Another method is the committee approach in which the problems are discussed and resolved in group discussion. One difficulty of this method is that of one person dominating the group although he or she is not the best linguist.

Pilot studies can also reveal conceptual difficulties implicit in problems of translation. Some words may be quite easy to translate, while others may need a phrase to express the idea. In these cases there is no problem about the conceptual equivalence of the idea, but in some cases the concept may be unique to the culture and have no exact equivalent in verbal terms in the other language. Whether this will mean that a more extensive examination of the concept will be needed or whether it should be omitted from the interview schedule will depend on how essential it is to the focus of the research.

The selection and training of interviewers for cross-cultural research frequently involves the use of speakers in each of the languages to be employed. It is not enough for these interviewers to be competent speakers in each of the relevant languages; they must also be able to carry out the interviews according to the research methodology. It is important to involve them in the pilot studies and translation procedures.

Cultural attitudes affecting interviewing in cross-cultural research

Interviewing across cultures, whether for research or other purposes, involves many aspects of communication apart from language (as will be discussed in more detail in chapter 13).

Interviewers selected must be acceptable to the culture. In many cultures the following actions are unacceptable.

- To send a woman to interview a man.
- To send a man to interview a woman.
- To interview a married woman alone.
- To interview a married woman without her husband being present.
- To send a person of one religion to interview a person of a different religion when factions from each are in conflict.
- To mention the names of recently deceased persons.
- To refer directly to matters which are tabu.
- To ask questions as the means of obtaining information.
- To make direct rather than circuitous replies.

- To look directly into a person's face when speaking.
- To respond in a manner which will cause the questioner to lose face.

These are but some examples. There are many individual and social-class based variations on how these behaviours would be tolerated. Younger respondents, those with higher education and those with experience with people of other cultures are less likely to keep to traditional cultural restrictions.

Gaining access

In many cultural contexts access to potential respondents may be restricted: the researchers and their assistants cannot simply approach a person and ask that person for an interview. In these cases researchers need to obtain the approval of leaders of the community before approaching individuals. Once this agreement is reached, cooperation will usually follow. Such approval is essential in many ethnic minorities who are wary of intrusion by researchers.

An important point to remember in making such contacts is to be sure that the right community leader or leaders are approached. If there is internal dissension within a community—be it religious, political, or disagreement over traditional rights—it is well to check carefully beforehand whom it will be best to approach. What may appear trivial to an outsider may have serious implications for relations within that ethnic or cultural community.

Feedback

It follows that after the research is completed, there is an obligation to provide feedback in the form of some kind of report to the community. If it is not practicable to contact the participants individually, then the report can be given to the community leaders.

SUMMARY

This chapter introduced the use of interviewing as the principal method of data collection in research. The reasons for choosing interviewing were given and the methods of carrying out studies were outlined. Particular attention was given to issues of reliability and validity, including the training of interviewers, coding of responses and content analysis. In discussing the use of interviewing in cross-cultural research, issues of particular importance were the comparability of concepts and functional equivalence of sampling, the content of interview schedules, the language used and problems of translation.

ACTIVITIES FOR STUDENTS

One of the best ways to learn how to use interviewing in research is to plan a small research project and carry it out for yourself.

Construct the questions using a number of different question formats and follow the steps discussed above. Check to see that you have kept on track, and that bias has not crept into your questions or into the way you interpreted the responses using the method of structural analysis set out in chapter 6.

You can do this in a cross-cultural framework, but beware of cultural differences in language and relationships between interviewer and respondents.

chapter

8

INTERVIEWING IN ORGANISATIONAL SETTINGS

Organisations employ interviewing in a wide variety of situations, including the simpler over-the-counter interviews, opinion polls and market research interviews referred to in chapter 2. The most frequent use of interviews relates to jobs, particularly personnel selection, appraisal and dismissal. As there is a vast research literature on these interviews and many of the findings are contradictory, we will need to limit this chapter to some of the major issues.

Personnel selection

The main focus of research on personnel selection interviews is on how efficient the interview is in predicting later performance. Most of this research literature suggests that the interview is not very successful in this respect. Reviews of studies (Aamodt, 1991; Statt, 1994; Ribeau & Poppleton, 1978; Herriot, 1991; Avery & Baker, 1990) in Britain and the United States of America show low correlations with later performance criteria, of the order $+.16$ to $+.23$. However, these authors all criticise the methodologies of at least some of the studies which were included in their surveys. As the information sought differed widely and many different types of jobs were included in these studies, Ribeau & Poppleton consider that it is not surprising that there is so little agreement and that the correlations are so low. Some improvement was shown when the interviews were structured, but judgements by a number of interviewers about the same applicants differed considerably.

If prediction validity is not a useful criterion, what other functions are served by the selection interview? The interview may show how well the interviewee will fit into the organisation. If this is the case, personal impressions will be used as much as predictions of performance.

A useful distinction has been made by Wernimont & Campbell (1968; cited in Statt, 1994) between signs and samples. Whereas samples of work such as a typing test or details from a curriculum vitae can provide evidence of past performance, signs are what are reacted to in the interview together with interpretations of personality and attributional traits gathered from such measures as psychological tests. The signs deriving from the interview lead to the interpretations the interviewers make of interviewees' behaviour at the time and how they judge the interviewee's personal qualities.

Research (Furnham, 1992; Aamodt, 1991; Argyle, 1992) has shown that first impressions are extremely powerful influences. Impressions are more favourable when the interviewee is most like the interviewer. Complex differences based on gender are reported: female interviewees are judged more favourably if they appear attractive with a feminine style of dress and appearance when the position is at a junior level; but when the position is at a higher level, they are likely to be judged less favourably than males, and personal attractiveness is less likely to be in their favour if they appear in feminine style of dress and appearance.

It is also suggested that the needs of the interviewers may be more important than the qualifications of the applicant. The representatives of the organisation feel a need to have some personal contact with whomever they are going to appoint. As the applicants who are interviewed are a small, select group culled from the larger pool of applicants, most of whom have already been excluded, the interviewers want to have some experience of interacting with the interviewees to judge their acceptability to themselves and their organisation. Research suggests that the decision is made within the first few minutes of the interview, and hence relies strongly on first impressions.

To counteract these problems, writers propose several methods to improve predictability and overcome subjective biasing factors.

Statt (1994) considers that the size of the interviewing panel should not be greater than two or three. The large panel is intimidating and no more reliable because of the many different interests represented.

There appears to be general agreement among these writers that the structured interview is more efficient in prediction than the unstructured interview. The structured interview should contain the same questions for each interviewee.

Multi methods using both signs and samples should be used where possible. These would include samples of previous work, data from psychological tests and scales, and providing precise information about the nature of the job and the organisation.

The performance appraisal interview

These interviews have two main functions: developmental and administrative. The developmental function is to provide feedback to the employee of strengths and weaknesses, and ways to improve performance. The administrative function is for management to evaluate an employee's performance. Appraisal interviews are also used when retrenchments are likely to follow a reorganisation and for decisions on salary increase. They occur after an employee has been working in the organisation for some time, but the time when they occur varies from one organisation to another.

- Aamodt (1991) recommends taking plenty of time with these appraisals, both in the preparation and the conduct of the interview.
- Moderate reports—for example, that an employee's performance was 'satisfactory'—were found (Aamodt, 1991) in the United States to lead to employee dissatisfaction.
- Reasons for any negative appraisal should be discussed.
- Employees should be allowed to give their own appraisal of their performance first.
- Positive feedback should be given first.
- Once problems are identified, the last stage is to seek solutions.

Multi methods using raters, objective criteria based on quantity of output and quality of work, and subjective scales such as critical incidents and employee comparison have all been used. Ribeau & Poppleton report that raters were more effective if they held a position that was not too high above the employee, whereas interview appraisers were more effective if they were higher in position than raters.

The dismissal interview

The problems inherent in these interviews are revealed in the number of terms which are used. They include such terms as 'separation', 'termination', 'letting go', 'retrenchment', and 'downsizing'. While many of the terms used by management tend to be euphemistic, the employee is more likely to think of them all as meaning 'Telling me I've got the sack'.

Unfortunately, in present times of change such interviews are all too frequent. Not only factory and office employees but many middle and senior management staff are retrenched in company takeovers and restructuring.

If the intention is to rid the organisation of the employee, is there any need to pay attention to this type of interview? There are several reasons: one reason might simply be the kindly attitude of the manager; another might be in order to maintain the good reputation of the company or organisation. The employee may have given the company good service, and there may be no complaints about the employee's personal qualities, motivation or performance. Or there may be a legal threat, and the intention is to avoid dealing with a union appealing against unfair dismissal.

If the person has been with the company for many years the relationship of trust and interdependence which has been built up over that time is abruptly threatened. For a person who is at middle-management level, or even at CEO (chief executive officer) level, the prospect of unemployment can be devastating, golden handshakes notwithstanding.

What interviewing methods can be used to alleviate the stress of such interviews?

Recognising the personal worth of the employee will be helpful, but these statements need to be sincere, otherwise they will create even more stress.

Showing a caring attitude for the person's future welfare will be a positive approach. This would include helping to find another position by contacting employment agencies, seeing that the employee has access to the maximum family welfare benefits and ensuring that the person knows how to obtain help.

When takeovers occur or the restructuring is implemented from the top management level, the interviewer given the task of conducting the termination interview is probably not personally responsible. However, although the argument that 'It's not my doing, it's the policy', may well be true, it is unlikely that the interviewee will view that argument favourably when the interviewer is still safe. This would seem, therefore, to be a somewhat doubtful tactic.

SUMMARY

Although interviewing is carried out in a range of activities in organisations, this chapter has been limited to the three most widely used: interviews for selection, performance appraisals and interviews when terminating employment. Research on the predictive ability of the selection interview suggests that the interview is not a good predictor of later performance; it appears, however, that other needs of the interviewing panel are often uppermost, such as a need to have some personal contact before the employee begins work. Ways of improving predictability are to link the interview content more closely to the task required, by using a combination of methods with samples of work and psychological tests. Ways of improving performance appraisal interviews suggested were to include the employee in the process and to follow up the evaluation with positive suggestions for improving performance. A caring attitude toward the employee's future needs as well as help in obtaining either another position or welfare entitlements were proposed as means to soften the impact of the dismissal interview.

ACTIVITIES FOR STUDENTS

Role-playing each of the three types of interview discussed will help to develop some empathy with the interviewers and respondents.

Try to ensure that you take a turn in the roles of both employer and applicant or employee.

Talk to someone of your acquaintance who has recently attended one of these interviews as the interviewee. What were this person's feelings? Was there something that was not asked, which the person felt should have been mentioned? If possible, also talk to someone who has been on a selection panel.

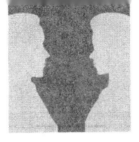

chapter

9

INTERVIEWING CHILDREN

When an adult interviews a child how does the child view the situation? Can an adult interviewer show empathy across the wide gulfs of age and experience? Can an interviewer rely on a young child's answer to questions? What kind of language should the interviewer use to communicate with a child respondent? These are some of the challenging issues we face in interviews with children. Yet, interviewing children can be a rewarding and enjoyable experience for both interviewer and child, and there is ample evidence that even young children can participate fully and give reliable responses. In this chapter we will show how to conduct interviews with children to elicit attitudes and levels of thinking (as in the research interview), and obtain information (as in the cognitive interview). Situations of severe stress such as trauma, child abuse and court evidence will be treated later (see chapter 15).

Putting yourself at the child's level

From the young child's viewpoint adults are enormous. Their view of adults is not of faces but of trousers, skirts and legs. To make contact the first rule is to physically come down to their level. You may have noticed how pre-school teachers spend a lot of their time bending down and squatting at the child's level. If you are not as flexible as that a chair will be needed, but it must be at the child's level. Practice in sitting on children's chairs will be necessary until you can feel comfortable. A tight or short skirt can be quite a problem!

Arranging the physical conditions

It is unfortunately true that interviews with children often have to be conducted in conditions which are improvised and not very private, such as in a school where the only room available is one which is big enough for thirty, or is the library or the gym. Despite this difficulty the interviewer must try to arrange the physical conditions to allow for comfortable seating, quietness and lack of interruptions. A small room in which interviewer and child are not distracted by other people coming and going is best. It is not necessary, and indeed probably a poor idea, to have the room decorated with many pictures and mobiles which will attract the child's attention. They may instead provide a distraction. Bright colours are fine but a fussy, busy decor should be avoided.

The furniture should suit the child rather than the interviewer. Chairs should be strong enough to hold an adult and an active child, and low enough for the child's feet to reach the floor comfortably. The height of the table also should be such that the child can easily view the stimulus materials and reach them if required. If the child is to hold, touch or manipulate them in any way, they should be sturdy enough to withstand rough treatment, safe to handle and free of toxic matter.

There should also be a place to put your own equipment out of sight when not in use. Another small table or chair may be adequate.

Something for the child to do

Many interviews with children take place within the context of some other task. For example, research testing of young children on cognitive tasks and concepts in social development is usually carried out individually. The task is presented and questions are asked about some aspect of the task's demands. Reasons for their responses may be sought. Clinical interviews with children also use activities as adjuncts to their questioning. Projective psychological tests all involve questioning about the pictures, dolls, puppets, and so on, which are presented.

When the interview is part of a total experience such as a research test-ing situation, the demands of the task will determine the characteristics of the activity. In this case the activity must represent the variables in a sys-tematic way. The development of the materials for the activity, the question format and the instructions are integral to the whole testing procedure. An example is given in the 'Interview with Joshua' at the end of this chapter (in which the child is interviewed about the distribution of rewards following events in the story-material used for the interview).

In this interview with Joshua, a four-year-old Chinese child, the fluidi-ty of this child's thinking about the issues is apparent. Previous work (Keats & Fang, 1996) had shown five-year-old Chinese children to be quite stable in their concepts; but, in contrast to the Australian children, some also gave preference to the youngest child, as Joshua did. This is in accord with the traditional teaching of looking after the youngest. Joshua was unable to articulate his reasoning and could agree on an equal distribution being fair but not the more advanced distribution which balanced effort and product with ability. Joshua's conceptual level in his responses to the final group of questions also shows this fluidity. He sees no conflict in claiming to be Chinese and also claiming to be Australian, but links his cultural identity to his language ability: the interviewer cannot be Chinese because she cannot speak Chinese. This is not unlike the situated identity concepts which Weinreich (1999) has found in older children and adolescents.

Less formally, a great range of activities can be used to anchor the ques-tioning. Doll play, puppets, pictures and stories, toys of various kinds, cars and models of houses, shopping baskets and sand play are all useful. Questions can be framed around videos and cartoons. Plasticene, crayons and paper to draw on—all provide valuable aids. The main thing to remem-ber is that the activity should be chosen carefully so that it can become an integral part of the interview and not simply be a distraction. Rapport built up by play activity beforehand must not be lost by removing the activity abruptly when the questioning actually begins.

Talking to children

Casual observation and one's own experience with younger relatives as well as the evidence of research into children's language acquisition (Brown, 1973) reveal that adults change their speech style when talking to young children. Baby talk to infants is followed by a form of simplified vocabulary and syntax used with toddlers. As the child learns language it begins to use a modified grammar which applies rules to verb forms as in 'John hitted the dog'.

Much has been written about this stage of the acquisition of language. By about five years of age a normally developing child has acquired all the basic grammar needed for conveying needs, expressing ideas and answering questions. This appears to be true whatever the native language (for many examples, see Munroe & Munroe, 1994).

Although the child's general level of language development has to be considered, it is not necessary for an interviewer to talk down to children. To convey one's meaning the language should be clear and plain. Long and complex sentence structures must be avoided. Asking one question at a time, simply expressed, will usually pose little difficulty. Avoid rhetorical questions. Check that the child knows the meaning of a word before asking questions based upon that term. There are many individual differences in language skills so it is important to make use of the introductory stages devoted to developing good rapport to find the appropriate language level.

Children's memory and understanding

How reliable is a child's reporting of an event compared with an adult's? This question is related to the problem of how easy it is to influence a child's responses. It is often claimed that, because the interviewer is likely to be in a position of greater power, children are more easily influenced than adults by leading questions. It is also claimed that children, because of their lesser cognitive development are more likely than adults to err in their memory of events. The research evidence does not support these contentions.

Research by Dent (1992) has shown that the age of the respondent is not as great an influence on changing testimony in the face of leading questions as other factors. Dent found that, although there was some increase in resistance in older children, the naivete of younger children helped to sustain their opinions whereas adults were more aware of the social implications and the need to be thought of favourably.

This research has also shown that young children's memory can be highly reliable, even in the face of leading questions suggesting contrary memories. The findings have particular significance for situations in which children have to give evidence in court (see chapter 15).

Children's imagination

The vividness and creativity of children's imagination can be a great boon in interviewing, especially when a child is asked to make up a story-type response to some activity material. For example, in sand play the figures may represent actual members of the family, real houses and pet animals along with space-warriors, space-ships and dinosaurs all in the one story.

This imaginative response should not be interpreted as memory failure or error. The interviewer's skill is to separate what is based on experience from what is fantasy and to bring the theme of the interview back on to the central stage without denigrating the child's fanciful narration, which would thereby show a rejection of the child's efforts.

Individual differences in temperament, in cognitive ability and in language skills all influence the child's imaginative ability.

Rewards

Whether a child should be offered a reward for participating in an interview is a contentious issue. On the one hand, it seems fair that the child should be given some reward for the effort put in; on the other, the promise of a reward can be seen as a bribe.

It would seem best to avoid making the child's cooperation contingent on receiving a reward later. This can so easily backfire. Consider the following example. You are interviewing two contrasting children who are asked the same questions relating to an incident at which both had been present. To gain their cooperation you promise a reward for answering your questions. You promise an even more attractive reward if they will tell you everything they can remember about what took place.

One child thinks only of getting the attractive reward, and answers confidently and fluently in the way she thinks most likely to please, irrespective of the accuracy of detail. Her story becomes more embellished as it grows. Will you give her the reward even when you realise what she is doing? Will you give it because she is being so helpful? Or will you withhold it because she is not telling the truth?

The other child is neither confident nor fluent. She tells her story hesitantly, making many false starts. The more mixed up she becomes, the more she sees the prospect of the reward disappearing until she loses confidence and ceases to go on. Will you give her a reward, and if so, which one? If you give it, will she think it unfairly given because she knows she did not give a good account of the incident as she remembered it? If you don't give it, will that not reinforce her feelings of inadequacy? Such a child can easily treat the interview as a test, and one in which she has failed.

If a reward is to be given, it should be given as a thank-you for the child's effort and for taking part, not for the quality of the performance, nor for the veracity of the responses. It would be much better to work carefully to develop good rapport at the beginning and ensure that the experience of taking part in the interview is enjoyable enough to be a reward in itself. You do not want to create a situation where the size of the reward has to be constantly enlarged to satisfy children's demands.

Duration

It is not possible to set time limits on interviews with children. Ten minutes can be quite a long time to a young child if the questioning is demanding, but if an absorbing activity is involved a much longer period can elapse before the child tires. How long a child can take part will depend on many factors, including the child's age, the difficulty of the topic and the environmental conditions which are likely to act to distract attention.

When the child begins to wriggle around in the chair and avoid eye contact it is probably an indication that the interview should soon draw to a close. A change of activity or topic may be sufficient to redirect the child's attention, but if the child is too tired the attention will not last. Give plenty of breaks. Wriggling may also mean that a toilet break is needed. Don't put that off too long for the sake of continuing with your interview. The child's concentration will be lost, and disaster may ensue.

SUMMARY

The focus of this chapter was on interviewing young children. The interviewer must be on the same level as the child, in the way the interviewer and child are seated and in understanding the level of the child's thinking and language. Many ways of combining the verbal questioning with activities which will appeal to the child were suggested, but it was stressed that these should be integrated into the main theme of the interview. The problems of offering rewards were considered.

ACTIVITIES FOR STUDENTS

To develop your interviewing skills with children, make up a small set of questions on a topic of interest which is suitable for children. Some possible questions might be on what they like about television, or what games they most like to play, or how children might help to improve the environment. To begin with, choose a topic which does not involve stressful interpersonal relationships.

You can work individually, in pairs or as a group.

You can choose to do this as a small study, in which case consult the chapter on research interviewing to help set up your interview schedule.

If you are only wanting to acquire some practical skills, it will still be valuable to prepare an interview schedule.

In either case you need to begin with a few children of a range of ages, say between five and twelve years.

To help you prepare the questions ask two children each aged five, seven, nine and twelve to tell you what they think your topic means.

Let them give you their own ideas. Observe the difference in the speech styles and conceptualisation across the age levels.

You will need to record what they say. Before you approach the child, make sure that your equipment is working and that you can record the answers. Try it out on a friend first.

Will you need some activity materials? Prepare them and the place in which they are to be used before you approach the children you are going to interview.

Try out your questions for your interview schedule with a friend or fellow student. Is there bias in the way the questions are phrased? Is the vocabulary too difficult? Are the sentences too long or too complex?

Now you are ready to interview. Do as many as you can with different age groups until you feel confident that you are comfortable with children and they are comfortable with you. This should be an enlightening and enjoyable exercise for both you and the children.

INTERVIEW WITH JOSHUA

Joshua is four years old. His Chinese given name is Han but when with Australians he uses Joshua as his name. He is the son of Chinese parents and has been in Australia for about two-and-a-half years. He speaks both Chinese and English and attends a pre-school and day-care centre. His parents also speak Chinese and English. Recently they took him to visit his grandparents in Chengdu, a large city in Sichwan Province, China.

The interview was carried out in Joshua's home. The 'Apples Story' was used as stimulus material for the interview. This story was created to examine, in Chinese and Australian children, the development of concepts of fairness in the giving of rewards. In the original study, which is reported in full in Keats & Fang (1996), the youngest children were five years of age. Parallel Chinese and Australian versions of the stimulus material were made with similar illustrations (except that hair colouring was different); the children were given Chinese names in the Chinese version and Australian names in the other one.

The story is about four children who help a poor farmer who becomes ill and is unable to pick the apples from his trees when they become ripe. The four children offer to help: a boy, Xaio Qiang; a girl, Li Li, a little younger; a much older boy, Xiao Tao; and Ming Ming, a much younger child. Xaio Qiang works very hard and at the end of the day has a large basket of apples. Li Li also works very hard and at the end of the day has a large basketful, too, although it is not quite as large as Xaio Qiang's. But Xiao Tao is lazy and, instead of working hard, chases butterflies and cicadas; at the end of the day he has only a small number of apples in his basket. Ming Ming works enthusiastically but of course cannot reach very high, and so picks up apples which fall, and at the end of the day has almost as many as Xiao Tao. The illustration shows the four children with their baskets of apples.

I: Joshua, I have a story for you. I hope you will like it. It's about some children and some apples. I'll ask you some questions about it. We have a tape-recorder to help me remember what we say. You can try it out if you like. Would you like to say something on the tape-recorder? [Joshua nods.]

I: Can you count up to 10?

J: Yes. I can count. [Counts to 10 in English.] I can count in Chinese too. [Counts to 10 in Chinese.]

I: Very good. Now we know it works. Joshua, I know that you went to China, didn't you? This story is about some children in China. Here it is, we've got some pictures, too.
[Interviewer tells the story showing the pictures and using the Chinese names.]

I: When the farmer saw that the children had helped, he felt much better and wanted to give them a reward. What do you think the farmer would give them as a reward?

J: Some apples

I: Yes, some apples. And here is a basket and here are the apples.
[Interviewer takes out a small basket and places in it eight bright red, plastic pencil-sharpeners in the shape of apples, to act as the apples.]

J: I didn't pick any ones.

I: Look at them, aren't they beautiful. You can count them. [Counts with Joshua.]

I: Now, how shall the farmer give those eight apples to the children so that it's fair? You put the apples out the way you think is fair. Do you know what 'fair' is?
[Joshua shakes his head.]

I: Well, 'fair' means it's good for everybody, just right.

J: Yes.

I: Now you take the apples and put them where you think they ought to go.
[Joshua gives four to the smallest child, Ming Ming, two each to the younger boy, Xaio Qiang, and girl, Li Li, and none to the biggest boy, Xiao Tao.]

I: Now he's got?

J: Four

I: And he's got?

J: Two

I: And she's got?

J: Two

I: And he's got?

J: None. [Joshua counts them out.]

I: Well, why did you give Xiao Tao none?

J: [Laughs] 'cause ... 'cause...

I: Why did you give Ming Ming four?

J: 'Cause I want to.

I: You want to. Right. Why did you want to?

J: 'Cause ... I thought about that.

I: What did you think?

J: I don't know.

I: Well, why did you give her two?

J: Because I want to.

I: Well, I think that looks very nice. But there are lots of other ways the farmer could give them out. What other way could you do it?

J: I don't know.

I: I'll show you a few more ways. What if we give him two, and her two, and him two and him two. [Interviewer places two apples on each child.] Would that be fair?

J: Yes.

I: It would? Why would that be fair?

J: 'Cause they all got the same.

I: Is that good?

J: Yes.

I: All right, I can tell you another way we could do it. What if we give Xaio Qiang [with most apples] three, and Li Li two, and we give Ming Ming two and Xiao Tao one. Would that be fair? [While speaking, Interviewer places the apples on each child.]
      [Joshua shakes his head.]

I: No? Why not?

J: He's only got one.

I: I see. Well, he didn't get so many. He's a big boy and he didn't get many. But it's not fair?
      [Joshua shakes his head.]

I: All right, let's try something else. What if we give him another one? [Interviewer takes one from Ming Ming and gives it to Xiao Tao.] Is that fair now?

J: No.

I: Why isn't it fair?

J: 'Cause that one's only got one.

I: Do you think the farmer was kind to give the apples to the children?

J: Yes.

I: If you had more apples, do you think the farmer could do better if he gave out all these apples? [Interviewer puts four more apples into the basket.]
      [Joshua gives out three apples each.]

I: Now they've all got the same. Are you happy with that?

J: Yes.

I: Do you like apples, Joshua?

J: Yes.

I: Where do you go to get apples?

J: You just buy them.

I: You just buy them. Where do you buy them?

J: At the shop.

[Further questions probed about shopping in China and Australia.
The final group of questions took up issues of cultural identity.]

I: When you went to China you saw your grandma and grandpa. They
      live in China. Are they Chinese?

J: Yes.

I: You live in Australia, are you Australian?

J: Yes.

I: Why are you Australian?

J: 'Cause I can speak English.

I: Are you Chinese?

J: Yes, 'cause I can speak Chinese.

I: Will you always be Chinese?

J: Yes.

I: Are your mummy and daddy Chinese?

J: Yes.

I: Can a person be a Chinese and be an Australian, too?

J: Yes. I can be a Chinese and I can be an Australian.

I: Can I be a Chinese?

J: No, because you can't speak Chinese.

chapter

10

INTERVIEWING ADOLESCENTS

For the purposes of this chapter the term 'adolescent' refers to young people roughly between the age of twelve and eighteen years. These ages are not to be taken as inflexibly defining the upper and lower age-limits of adolescence. Adolescence is a stage of development rather than a specific age range: early maturing girls and later maturing boys are to be found in the same school classes as later maturing girls and earlier maturing boys. The age of eighteen is the age at which one can vote as an adult, but many eighteen-year-olds are at school. At the lower end of the range, the shift from the atmosphere of the primary school to that of the high (or secondary) school at the age of around twelve is a change of great significance: they are beginning high school as the youngest and least important there, compared to having been in the highest and most responsible year when in their final year at primary school.

The social environments and values of family, school and peer group interact powerfully in their influence upon the adolescent. Relationships with these referent others can be quite stressful for many adolescents, while for others there appears to be little conflict between the values of these three groups.

Generally, the life of adolescents can become extremely complex. A very large number of adolescents have to cope with various problems—of being in single-parent families, of the break-up of their families by divorce and the building of new relationships with step-families—apart from the pressures of schooling and the demands of meeting the norms of the peer group. It is not surprising, therefore, that many of the contexts in which adolescents are interviewed are situations in which the adolescent is present because of some problem.

The situation of those who do not do well in school and are not motivated toward school achievement is made more difficult by the fact that the traditional alternative of leaving school to take a job at the earliest date the legal school-leaving age will allow is now no longer available in the present state of high youth unemployment. Many of those who do leave school find themselves without a job, with no money and few opportunities.

For the students who do perform well the school environment provides support and boosts motivation but also creates high levels of competitive stress, especially in the final years when the students' aims are to gain entry into tertiary studies. There are few senior high-school students who do not feel such pressure.

Excerpts from the transcripts of interviews with two adolescents are given at the end of this chapter (the interview with Adam, and the interview with Carlie). Both these young people are articulate and are doing well in school. The contrast between the younger and the older respondent is very evident: there are the pressures of higher level studies for the sixteen-year-old and there is the newness of the high-school experience in the twelve-year-old respondent. Although the topic is the same for both of these adolescents, the differences in their maturity of conceptualisation, in their language styles and in their concerns and social relations are readily apparent.

Much research has been carried out on adolescents' coping skills (for example, Frydenberg & Lewis, 1994), their self-esteem and self-concept (Gibson, Westwood, Ishiyama, Borgen et al., 1991), and the attitudes of youth to social issues such as unemployment (Feather, 1998). Because adolescence is also a time of questioning and thinking about the self and one's role in society now and in the future, many studies of adolescent concerns, interests and attitudes have been conducted. Interviews on these topics reveal many insights into adolescent thinking. Focus-group interviews are often used to obtain adolescent views on such topics. Cross-cultural research also has addressed the concerns of adolescents (Gibson, Westwood, Ishiyama, Borgen et al., 1991; Kornadt, Hayashi, Tachibana, Trommsdorff & Yamauchi, 1992).

In immigrant families the intergenerational differences which occur within most families are also affected by the differences between demands of the adolescents' peer environment, the school and home. Ghuman (1999) gives many examples from interviews in his research with adolescents of

South Asian and Chinese background in the United Kingdom. For example, a Muslim father is unhappy with his daughter attending mixed schools, and a school principal is concerned that, while in the school the emphasis is on teaching girls to be independent and critical thinkers, at home they are taught the virtues of collective responsibility and unquestioning respect to the elders of the family.

Language of adolescents

Two aspects are of particular relevance for interviews with adolescents: the first is their ability to understand and use language, the second is the use of the speech styles they adopt to express themselves.

Together with the wide range of physical development there is also an equally wide range of cognitive and personality development. Linguistic ability is well-developed among adolescents, although some are better able to express their ideas than others. Social differences in language style can appear to obscure thinking in those with poorer language competence. However, perhaps the biggest problem for adult interviewers is not that teenagers lack the ability to express themselves but that the current popular language of the teenager is almost a foreign language to many adults. It is almost impossible for an adult to keep up to date with teenagers' shared language. Adults who are not closely involved with the youth culture will soon find their ignorance revealed.

In many ways this language has a similar function to the 'secret languages' made up by children in play and to communicate with close friends or siblings. It is intended to keep adults uninformed as much as to communicate amongst themselves. The language of adolescents contrasts with that of younger children in that it is highly influenced by advertising and the peer group culture.

Adolescents can be extremely sensitive to adult hypocrisy. An adolescent will quickly see through adults' attempts to use adolescents' language styles for their own ends. To try to emulate their language styles for the sake of developing good rapport, to appear to be more like the adolescent, is not likely to succeed. However, it is very likely that the adult interviewer will fail to understand many terms used by adolescent respondents. In this case it will be necessary to ask for clarification, but only if the interviewer genuinely both wants and needs to know.

Appearance

Like their language styles, adolescents' dress and hairstyles are likely to present an appearance which may belie their attitudes and abilities. Beware of attributing an untidy mind to an untidy teenage dresser. Fashions are extremely changeable and strongly influenced by peer group pressure.

Young people going for job interviews are often advised on how to present themselves to create the best impression. Generally, this means to dress more formally and conservatively than they normally would. Some do take that advice, but the more individualistic, who do not want to be straightjacketed into conventional behaviour, may resist the advice and not change their way of dressing. An interviewing panel will, of course, have its agenda for the requirements of the job; the question its members must face is whether the appearance of the applicant is a more important consideration for the job than the attitudes or skills required. In any case, with the present situation of high youth unemployment many young job applicants cannot afford to dress up for each job interview.

Non-verbal behaviour

As with appearance, there are fashions in non-verbal behaviour as well as cultural, gender and age differences. Teenagers can be very expressive in their body language, especially when emotional involvement is high. Gestures may seem exaggerated in the eyes of adults.

Rapport

Achieving empathy between an interviewer and an adolescent respondent may be difficult for some interviewers who have had little experience with young people. Apart from the matters of language and appearance discussed above, their interests and lifestyles may also be so different as to be hard to understand. Students who are in their twenties will probably recall how difficult it was to interest older adults in whatever their own preoccupations were when they were teenagers.

However, if the interview topic is of mutual concern, and the interviewer genuinely wants the opinion of the adolescent respondent, the relationship can become very rewarding. How then can rapport be developed? The important condition is to establish one's credentials truthfully from the start and not to depart from that position as the interview proceeds.

Effects of uneven growth-patterns on responses

The maturity in some aspects of adolescents' lives and their later development in other aspects leads to much variability in response patterns. Some unpredictability in responses can also be expected. Emotions related to sexual awareness, self concept and self-esteem, and anxieties about school performance may affect the overall presentation, producing an uneven pattern of highs and lows and an exaggerated style of expression of feelings and attitudes.

Adjusting to the conceptual level

The conceptual ability of high-performing adolescents is certainly higher than that of most adults, although they may lack the breadth and depth of adult experience. However, school performance is not a good indicator of conceptual ability for those students whose motivation is low. Emotional highs and lows affect conceptual performance in interviews in students whether they are high-performing or low-performing at school. The interviewer must take into account more factors than school performance in adapting the phrasing and conceptual level of the questions to an individual respondent.

Making use of complex structures

All the individual differences and features of adolescent response styles suggest that their responses to questions will be likely to produce complex structures. The highly eloquent respondent will be able to give complex answers which will need to be followed up with probing and feedback loops to elicit the full wealth of meaning. The emotive respondent will also produce a complex structure as the interviewer attempts to unravel the mixed-up incoherent answers with probing and feedback loops. The taciturn respondent who is not linguistically skilled will also need help by probing in order to elicit a full response.

The need to be treated as adults

Above all, adolescents do not want to be treated as children. Because of the unevenness of adolescent growth to maturity, it will appear that in some situations they may behave as children or as if they would like the security of childhood. This behaviour may manifest itself in the course of the interview if the questions become threatening. A change of questioning style will then be needed to restore their sense of self-worth and acceptance.

SUMMARY

In considering the differences between interviewing young children and adolescents the great variability in growth patterns meant that many young people of the same age would differ in social and intellectual maturity. The problems of many young people in coping with the pressures of schooling, family and peer relations are likely to create the need for the interviewer to pay attention to building and maintaining the adolescent respondent's sense of self-worth and acceptance.

ACTIVITIES FOR STUDENTS

Using the same method you used for young children, choose a topic of interest by first asking a few teenagers about their interests and concerns.

Work out some questions with a fellow student.

Try these questions out with two respondents each 12, 15 and 17 years of age. Parental approval will be needed.

With one boy and one girl at each age level, interview as many as you can.

As before, you can do this individually or as a group exercise, putting the results together.

Observe the non-verbal behaviour carefully. If possible, use a video recorder but if that is not available tape-record the interview and make careful notes of the behaviour that accompanies the verbal responses.

Note the way you adapt your style to the three age levels.

INTERVIEW WITH ADAM

Adam is sixteen, the younger of two brothers. He is in the second last year (year 11) of high school and has a very good school academic record.

The following excerpts are from a longer interview which also included questions about his leisure interests and friends.

The interview was tape-recorded and the transcript is published with permission of Adam and his parents.

EXCERPT 1
ATTITUDES TO SCHOOL

I: What subjects are you doing this year, Adam?

A: Physics, 2-Unit Maths, General English, Legal Studies and Ancient History.

I: That seems a very broad-based program. Is it in a science stream or a general stream, or what?

A: No, it's just a mixture.

I: What do you think of school this year?

A: Oh, it's a lot harder.

I: What's harder about it?

A: Oh, ... I don't know really ... [Laughs]

I: Well, what do you like least about it?

A: All the work.

I: You said it was a lot harder. In what respect is it harder?

A: A lot more work.

I: Is it harder because there's a lot more work or because it's more difficult?

A: A bit of both.

I: How are you getting on?

A: Pretty well.

EXCERPT 2
SELF CONCEPT

I: Adam, if you were wanting to describe yourself to a boy in another country, say on the Internet or if you wanted to be a pen-friend, how would you describe yourself?

A: [Pause] ... Quiet ... I don't really know ...

I: Well, you know how these chat shows work, don't you? You're skilful with computers, I suppose ...

A: [Laughs] Not very!

I: Say you were interested in taking part in some kind of communication with a friend from another country and they asked you what you were like, what would you be able to say to them? Apart from 'I'm sixteen and I'm in year 11 and I can do Tae-kwon-do?'

A: Oh, I don't know, just that I'm quiet.

EXCERPT 3
CULTURAL KNOWLEDGE, INTERACTIONS AND ATTITUDES

I: In Australia to-day we have people who come from many different countries and cultural backgrounds. Do you know what I mean by 'cultural backgrounds'?

A: Yeah, their country's beliefs, like their religion, their monetary system, things like that.

I: Yes. Do you have any friends who have cultural backgrounds that are different from yours?

A: Yes, I've got some Italian friends.

I: Are they from school?

A: Yes.

I: And what sort of things do you do together?

A: Well, sometimes play basketball.

I: Do you always get along well together?

A: Yep.

I: How is that?

A: Just good friendship, it's no different really.

I: No different. If someone asked you what is your cultural identity, what would you say?

A: I'm Australian ... [Laughs]

I: Australian ... What would that mean?

A: I don't really know ... just ... [Laughs]

I: Well, if you take the Italian friends of yours, have they been here for a long time?

A: Yes.

I: What about those who come from other countries? For example, at present the Serb population here is in the news a lot.

A: Yeah.

I: Could you be a Serb and an Australian at the same time?

A: [Pause] ... No, because of their religious beliefs and their different political beliefs.

I: But would that stop you from seeing yourself as both a Serb and an Australian?

A: I suppose not.

I: Why not?

A: Well they live in Australia and they're Australian citizens.

I: Some people think that that is a difficulty

A: Mm ...

I: and it's hard to be two people of different cultural backgrounds.

A: Mm ...

I: Have you ever thought about that before?

A: No. [Laughs]

I: Do you think it's a good thing or not so good to have so many people of different cultural backgrounds in Australia?

A: I think it's good.

I: Why do you think that?

A: Well, you get a taste of everything, like experiencing what other people eat, their views and their beliefs.

I: What other beliefs have you experienced and found different with your Italian friends?

A: Well, they have a lot more religious background and believe a lot more in God and stuff like that, and they're very close to their family.

I: Have you met any of their family?

A: A few, yes.

I: Is it very different from your family?

A: Yes, it's a bit different. They seem to spend a lot more time together, and they're closer kind of thing ...

EXCERPT 4

FUTURE PERSPECTIVES

I: There's a lot of talk now about the year 2000. I'd like to ask you now some questions about what you think the future will be like in the next century. What will your life be like in, say, five years time?

A: Well, I'll probably be working somewhere.
I: Five years from now ... can you think that far ahead?
A: Not really.
I: For you personally ... How old will you be, twenty-one?
A: Yes.
I: What would you have done by then?
A: I don't really know.
I: What do you think's ahead of you next year, the HSC?
A: Yes.
I: And after that?
A: I haven't planned that far.
I: Have you planned to go to university? You've got a good school record.
A: I don't know yet.
I: What about other people the same age as yourself? Are they thinking about the future at all?
A: I don't think anyone thinks about the future.
I: You don't?
A: No, not much.
I: Why is that?
A: Well they just want to get on with what's going on now, concentrate on school and stuff like that.

[After some questions on possible local changes, the questions asked about Australia generally.]

I: Do you think there will be a big change in Australia in the next five years?
A: No, not too big a change.
I: Why not?
A: It takes quite a long time for a change to happen really. Nothing drastic will happen.
I: What about after the Olympic Games? Will that make a difference?
A: It will during the Olympic Games, the population might rise a bit.
I: And after that?
A: The same.

EXCERPT 5
ADOLESCENTS' CONCERNS
I: What do you think are the main concerns that young people of your age have at present? What are the main things that interest them?
A: Well, getting through school is one of the main things you're worried about. Having fun with their friends and stuff.

I:	What other things do they worry about?
A:	What other people think about them.
I:	Could you tell me more about that?
A:	Well, they just want to make sure their image is what they want it to be like, that the people think right things about them. They don't want people thinking they're not good or something like that.
I:	What do you mean by 'not good'?
A:	Oh, losers or something like that.

EXCERPT 6
ADULTS' PERCEPTIONS OF ADOLESCENTS
I:	What do you think most adults think about young people of your age?
A:	Well, I don't really know.
I:	Don't know? [Adam laughs.] Well, some people have pretty strong ideas about teenagers, what they're like and what they do.
A:	Yeah.
I:	What sort of things do they think about them?
A:	Well they think that we're no good, or troublemakers or something.
I:	Do you think that's fair?
A:	No, not really.
I:	Why not?
A:	Because it's basically not true.

INTERVIEW WITH CARLIE

Carlie is twelve, she has two older sisters and one younger brother. She is in her first year (year 7) at high school, having come from a nearby primary school. Like Adam, she has an excellent school academic record. Her out-of-school interests are netball and dancing class.

The following are excerpts from a longer interview using the same schedule as for Adam. The interview was taped in the home. Permission to publish these excerpts has been given by Carlie and her parents.

EXCERPT 1
ATTITUDES TO SCHOOL
I:	Do you like it at this school?
C:	Yeah, it's all right.
I:	What do you like most about it?
C:	Recess and lunch.
I:	[Laughs] Why is that?
C:	Because there's no teachers around. And because my friends are all in different classes so I don't get to see them in class.
I:	Oh, yes, it's not like primary school where you're all in the same class. And what do you like least about it?

C: Umm ... Assembly.

I: Why is that?

C: Because the teachers they just ... it gets really boring and everybody's crammed in together and we have to sit on the floor ... They tell us what's happening in the week and if there's a special thing like when we have our year meetings ... and stuff like that.

I: Do you like high school compared with primary school?

C: Well, some things are not as boring because there were, like, a couple of slow people in my class, but all right, I'm not saying I can't agree that ... but there are some people who are sort of like that. I can't say it doesn't matter, but things are evening out. They're a little bit more challenging.

EXCERPT 2
SELF CONCEPT

I: If you wanted to describe yourself to another girl in another country, say on the internet or want to be a pen-friend, how would you describe yourself?

C: Umm ... Sometimes I can be bossy, ... umm ... I can be moody some-times, but I can like to listen a lot, and if, like, something bad hap-pened, well I can look at it and if I think, well you're in the right, I'll help you get it right. I'm twelve and all that sort of stuff.

EXCERPT 3
CULTURAL KNOWLEDGE, INTERACTIONS AND ATTITUDES

I: In Australia today we have many people who come from different countries with very different cultural backgrounds. Do you know what I mean by 'cultural backgrounds'?

C: Yes.

I: What would you say that means?

C: Well they, like, where they come from, they do things differently from how we do things.

I: What sort of things?

C: Like ... they ... the grandparents raise children until, like, a certain age and then they go to the parents or something. And, like, in some countries where it is not very free, like, women are not allowed to do things that we can do here and that sort of stuff.

I: Would that be true for girls as well as grown-ups?

C: Yes.

I: What sort of things?

C: Like, umm ... like ... girls don't play soccer in some countries.

[Some questions followed about whether she had any friends of a different cultural background. A friend from primary school is mentioned but went to a different high school.]

I: What did you do with your friend when you knew her?

C: Just what I do with my normal friends who are Australian.

I: What is that?

C: Eat lunch and talk and walk around.

I: If someone asked you what was your cultural identity, what would you say?

C: Australian. White Australian.

I: White Australian, is that all?

C: Yes, basically, yes.

I: Well, you mentioned your friend, and from what you said she is Chinese. Can you be a Chinese and an Australian too?

C: I think you can but ... I think that sometimes, like, people after someone dies, how the way they mourn forever and they're always in black and that ... I think, well, like, you do go through a stage but sometimes the way they do it, how they go on and on and ... and ... actually they're now in Australia they force that on their kids. I think, well, if you're in Australia you should, like, take your time and then get over it and not go on forever. Because you're in Australia now.

I: Do you think it's a good thing or not so good to have people of so many different cultural backgrounds in Australia?

C: Well I don't think it's a problem but I think if they come to Australia to live because they think it's a good place they should try and do more things like we do instead of, like, I mean sometimes the things they bring in, some of their culture's all right but then they're in Australia so they should try and be more like our stuff instead of trying to go getting us to do their stuff.

I: I think I am following you but I'd like you to tell me a bit more about what are the good things they should bring and what are the things that they should be more like Australia in. Start with the good things.

C: [Pause] ... Like, their different foods. I don't know ... Like, some people might like the way they dress on different occasions. But then I'd say what are the bad things would be like the way they believe in all their evil spirits. But I mean I know that's their thing but when they've got everything else, like, they've got everything, but when they start pushing that upon other people like the children, and then they start getting the people around to do it too I don't think, like, they should because it's not really what we believe in.

I: Do you think we should try to get them to believe in what we believe in?

C: Well, I think they should try to understand us more instead of us trying to get to understand them more.

EXCERPT 4
FUTURE PERSPECTIVES

I: There's a lot of talk around lately about the year 2000 and the next century. Everyone's talking about it, aren't they?

C: Yeah.

I: Do you think things will be different? I'd like to ask you some questions about what you think the future will be like next century.

C: Probably we'll have more advanced technology. Computers would have been replaced by then. TV will be totally different. We probably won't have pets like we do because we'll probably've destroyed our dogs by then.

I: Why do you think that would happen?

C: Because they're just going too fast in technology in, like, areas that are already, like, speeding instead of ... I think they could do more in medical technology than they do, instead of updating computers and making them dearer and dearer.

I: But aren't they getting cheaper?

C: The old ones are but not the more advanced ones.

[Interviewer then asked Carlie what her own future would be like in five years time.]

C: I'll be seventeen. Hopefully I'll be on my P (probationary driving) plates driving around in a car. I think I'll still be talking to my friends ... I'll still be at school.

I: And what do you think it will be like for other young people of your age?

C: Well, I think it would depend on if your family was wealthy enough to keep up with the technology or whatever's going around.

EXCERPT 5
ADOLESCENTS' CONCERNS

I: What do you think are the main concerns of young people of your age?

C: Well, there are a lot of people who worry about their weight.

I: Twelve year olds?

C: Yeah, there's people who walk around the school saying 'I'm too fat, I'm too fat' or 'I'm too thin, I'm too thin'. And people starting to worry about girl friends and boy friends, and ... some people want to be great, coolest or best and they keep changing their looks to try and look better for other people.

EXCERPT 6

ADULTS' PERCEPTIONS OF ADOLESCENTS

I: What do you think most adults think about young people of your age?

C: They don't really have any idea about what they're talking about.

I: Why do you say that?

C: 'Cause if they're there all the time and you're talking to people and they're talking about something and you say something they don't believe you, but with me if I said that, they don't believe it but it adds up that I always end up right. [Carlie gives an example from an incident when she was four years old which had a lasting impression.]

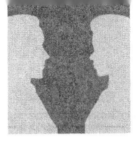

chapter

INTERVIEWING
THE AGED

A relatively young person can probably look back easily enough and remember what it was like to be an adolescent, but how easy is it for a young person to imagine what it would be like to be old, instead? Far more has happened in the lives of the elderly than they themselves could have imagined when they were young. To interview people of advanced age can be a wonderful experience if you approach it carefully. Nevertheless, there can be some problems for a relatively young interviewer.

Before we begin to consider the problems, first ask yourself, 'How old is old?', 'How old is middle-aged?'. Life-expectation figures published by the Australian Commonwealth Bureau of Statistics (1998) show that, at seventy years of age, people expected to live until their eighties, while at eighty they expected to be still around in their nineties. There are those who wind-surf at eighty, and many people sail in their nineties. A colleague's seven-year-old son, asked by his parents about his new teacher, said that he was tall, had brown hair and was middle-aged. The teacher was actually twenty-five years old. The perception of age, as of youth, is relative.

If this is the case, what is different about interviewing old people? Can we not treat them the same as any other adults? In many respects we can, and should, but there are some important constraints which need to be taken into account. For this chapter we will have to consider some of the physical frailties which affect the way many older persons will interact with an interviewer. In some cases some loss of mental function has to be accommodated.

If the interviewer is young, the difference in experience can create a problem with some respondents. They also can have a relative perception of age: to a ninety-year-old, a person of sixty can be treated as young; an interviewer in his or her twenties can be regarded as very young indeed.

Uses of the interview with old people

Because of the recent increase in the proportion of the population that is over sixty-five years of age, the need for research on the aged is also increasing. There is also an increasing demand by various social agencies, both government and private, for information about their needs and personal lifestyles (Drever, 1998).

Interviewing is a more effective way of obtaining data from many old people than expecting them to provide written responses. For their part, many old people do not like to be asked to fill in questionnaires. Their reasons include a lack of familiarity with written questionnaires, difficulty in reading, especially anything in small print, a lack of patience with the simplistic approach of some questionnaires, and because of their frailty in writing.

On the one hand, an interview allows the interviewer to be much more confident about the responses because of the opportunity for probing to amplify and verify. On the other hand, and more importantly from the respondent's point of view, the interaction with the respondent can be a pleasant social interlude. For older people who live alone or are in nursing homes, an interview with a receptive person offers companionship and stimulation, however transitory.

Some retirement villages and nursing homes have few opportunities for residents' social life; others have too many, with little privacy. In hostels, communal living conditions with other residents who are incompatible socially or who are showing signs of physical or mental deterioration can arouse anxiety.

Research with the aged

Although research on the aged has increased greatly in recent years, led particularly by the work of Baltes and his associates (Baltes & Baltes, 1990), it has been asserted, for example by Koder & Ferguson (1998) and Drever (1998) that Australian psychologists have not become as involved in this work as is needed by the community. Nevertheless, research on memory by

Luszcz (1992) and Luszcz & Hinton (1995) has shown not only task specificity but also improvements in memory self-efficacy with added experience. Older adults remembered less well than young-old, but they also improved. Educational background and initial levels of self-efficacy were important predictors of the improved performance.

To encourage research and help redress the former imbalance, the *Australian Psychologist* (1999) has brought together a Special Issue on 'Psychology and the Older Person'. Among the wide range of topics, two of particular relevance to the use of interviewing are the study by Thomas (1999) of stress, coping and mental health in two hundred older Vietnamese migrants, and the study of turning points in the lives of midlife and older women by Leonard and Burns (1999).

Thomas's study combined the administration of a number of psychological scales with interviewing. The scales were prepared and administered in the Vietnamese language and the interviews conducted by native Vietnamese speakers. There was some difficulty with the use of scales of the Likert type. Thomas comments (p. 83), 'Experience with elderly subjects suggests that they do not cope well with Likert scales, so the scoring of the measures was a Yes/No response with an open-ended question administered by Vietnamese-speaking interviewers'. The value of interviewing compared with using written responses only is apparent with these respondents even though all the materials were carefully prepared in the respondents' own language.

PROBLEMS IN INTERVIEWING

Hearing loss

Impaired hearing is very common, especially minor hearing difficulties. One ear may be bettter than the other. Hearing aids are often not used because of the interference of background noise. Some people may not admit to hearing loss, others will feign poor hearing when they do not want to answer the question. A preliminary check before the interview begins will be a useful precaution. Speak clearly, separating the words rather than letting them run together. Try to choose a location in which background noises, especially other voices, are minimised.

Eyesight

It is more likely than not that the respondent wears glasses. You may need to find out, before any written or pictorial materials are to be used, whether glasses are only needed for close work and reading or whether there is more general loss. If the interview requires any written materials, make sure that they are in large print.

Language

The language style of an elderly respondent may differ considerably from that of a young interviewer. Avoid neologisms, colloquialisms and slang. Unless there is evidence of cognitive impairment and hearing loss, careful, clear wording will generally be sufficient to be understood. However, a physically frail respondent may show some hesitancy and be slow of speech.

Mobility

For many old people, apart from their being just a little slower, lack of mobility is usually not a problem. However, for others confined to a wheel-chair or to bed in nursing homes, the interviewer will need to ensure that the physical setting is comfortable for both interviewer and respondent.

Use of equipment

If recording equipment is to be used there must be space enough to handle it and the interview schedule without everything falling about. Check the physical setting carefully before you begin. Also check that the respondent is familiar with methods of recording if tape- or video-recording is to be used.

Privacy

The topic of the interview will need to be selected according to whether a highly personal response is essential or not. Will privacy be essential? In hostels and nursing homes it may be a problem to find a suitably private location. If the interview has to be conducted with staff coming and going or with neighbours listening in a nearby bed or chair, the interview is unlikely to be able to deal with very personal matters.

Memory loss

Poor memory for names is a common failing in the elderly. They may have a better recall of events that took place in the distant past than of those that are more recent. Their memory can also be selective, discarding what they do not want to remember.

Empathy and sympathy

Respect and politeness are essential in gaining and maintaining rapport. A more formal approach than with a younger person may be needed, especially in the use of the person's name, where presumptions of familiarity will not be well-received. The aged do not want condescension, especially from the young who are so lacking in their experience. Attempts at understanding in an empathetic manner will be appreciated, although the older person may be quick to point out the interviewer's lack of knowledge at the same time as enjoying the company. Be prepared to reciprocate by responding to the social demands of the occasion. Cultural differences in the respect for the elderly should always be taken into account.

Patience

Plan enough time for the interview. Do not rush the respondent. Be patient with slowness, whether in responses, speech or mobility.

Keep to your structure

Some respondents may treat the interview as a social occasion which provides an opportunity to talk about their own interests instead of answering the interviewer's questions. In this situation it is very easy to allow the structure of the interview to be deflected into the channelling pattern of figure 5.3. Use the feedback loops and probing of the complex structure of figure 5.5 to get back on track (see figures in chapter 5).

Non-verbal reactions of the interviewer

The initial reactions of inexperienced interviewers meeting for the first time with really old people frequently reveal discomfort. They may feel repelled and disturbed by the old person's appearance. Although they may try to hide their feelings, the non-verbal response is not lost on many old people. It is important to concentrate on other aspects of the interaction and not allow oneself to show reactions non-verbally which contradict the message of the words being used to cultivate rapport.

SUMMARY

This chapter drew attention to some of the problems for interviewers of older people such as impaired hearing and vision, different language styles, problems of restricted mobility in the very frail and handicapped, lack of privacy in hostels and nursing homes and memory loss. Ways of coping with these problems were suggested. It was also pointed out that the experience of the interview could be an enjoyable one for both interviewer and respondent. The interviewer's respect for the older person's wealth of life experiences is essential for a good relationship.

ACTIVITIES FOR STUDENTS

The first step is to become more familiar with old people.

Go and visit someone in a nursing home, and someone in his or her own home. Do this as often as you can until you feel confident about meeting and talking informally with old people.

Take a part-time volunteer job or placement involving old people as part of your training.

In your class group prepare a set of photographs of old people in a variety of contexts, of differing ages and with various types of physical appearance.

Also prepare a set of questions to be asked about each person in the photographs. For example, What is this person doing? How old do you think this person is? What do you think about this person's appearance?

Show the photographs on overhead projections. If possible, video-tape the reactions of the observers. Examine your own reactions. To what extent did your non-verbal reaction match your verbal response to the photographs?

You can do this with a fellow student or as a class group.

Prepare a set of questions and try out your interviewing skills with a small number of respondents. Use a tape-recorder and review your performance afterwards. If practicable, use a video-camera and work in pairs with a fellow student.

chapter

12

INTERVIEWING PEOPLE WITH DISABILITIES

Whether your future work is as a psychologist, social worker, nurse, special education teacher, or in any other caring profession, you may have to interview people who have some type of physical or intellectual disability. The interview can stand alone with the single function of obtaining information, or be used in conjunction with, or as part of a program of intervention which includes diagnosis, testing, therapy and evaluation. In both cases you will need to relate to your respondent in supportive ways which will encourage effective responses to your questions.

This chapter will not be about counselling or therapy, or about the management of disabilities. For reference to these aspects there are many sources to consult. Of particular relevance to the understanding of people with disabilities there are the following publications: *Living with Disabilities* (Gething, Healy, Cutler, Geniale, Lean-Fore & Walker, 1984), and the later, more extensive volume, *Person to Person* (Gething, 1997). This later publication, based on the work of the Cumberland Disability Education Programme (CDEP), covers general concepts and attitudes to, and by people with hearing and visual impairment, spinal chord injury, cerebral palsy, epilepsy, intellectual impairment, amputation and short stature.

Here we will consider only how to ask questions in the situations of their daily lives. Problems and techniques for interviewing respondents in five groups of disability are discussed: acquired physical handicaps, congenital physical disabilities, sensory and perceptual disabilities, intellectual impairment, and multiple physical and intellectual disability.

Acquired physical handicaps

Under this heading are included disabilities such as paraplegia, which have come about from a traumatic event (a road accident or sport injury, for example), and the slower loss of physical functioning which results from a debilitating illness (such as motor neurone disease).

The extent to which physical function is impaired varies greatly: in some cases speech and language will be affected while in others a verbal exchange will present no communication problems. The interviewer will need to adapt according to the degree and nature of the disability, but other factors also need attention. The duration of the disability, the age of the respondent, and the environment in which the interview is to be conducted all have to be taken into account. It is not possible here to deal with specific cases; our aim is rather to try to create an attitude in interviewers which will facilitate rapport and encourage the fullest responses possible.

From the respondent's point of view, a supportive attitude is one which treats the person as an individual rather than as a type such as a 'paraplegic' or 'quadriplegic'. From the interviewer's standpoint, the important demand is to look beyond the physical state into the individual thinking and personality of the respondent. Condescending sympathetic expressions will be met with resistance; aggression which cannot find an outlet physically will turn into non-cooperation. It is always more effective to put the emphasis on what the person can do than what cannot be done.

Congenital physical disabilities

Typical examples of congenital physical disabilities are congenital limb deformity and cerebral palsy. The former includes physical deformities such as club foot and the malformations associated with thalidomide. Cerebral palsy is brought about by impairment of the neuromotor control areas of the brain and can involve a range of mild to severe problems of motor functioning. These may or may not be accompanied by intellectual impairment.

Gething, Healy, Cutler, Geniale, Lean-Fore & Walker (1984, p79) provides the following descriptions:

Spasticity	involuntary contractions of limb muscles causing awkward positions of the body.
Atheosis	constant involuntary worm-like movements of the limbs, trunk and face.
Ataxia	lack of co-ordination with clumsy gait and poor balance.
Atonia	muscle weakness causing difficulty in movement.
Mixed	a combination of two or more of the above.

Different congenital physical disabilities will affect an interview in considerably different ways. The presence of a congenital limb deformity, for example, may have no effect on a respondent's speech or intellectual functioning. In many cases the person has learned to adapt their motor behaviour to make best use of the limited functions. In some instances specially designed household equipment helps to facilitate normal social behaviour. However, the interviewer should be alert to the possible effects of the disability on the respondent's self-concept. Some who feel anxious regarding their appearance and acceptance by others may be apprehensive about the interviewer's attitudes.

The case of cerebral palsy is more complex, on the other hand. Communication may be a serious problem. Because the muscles controlling speech do not function properly, speech is often slurred and slow. This speech problem leads many people to regard the person as intellectually impaired. This is a very dangerous assumption. In fact, there is a wide range of intellectual capacity among people with cerebral palsy. Because of protective parental environments, people with cerebral palsy are often not allowed to extend themselves to their full developmental potential. The interviewer should, therefore, not make hasty judgements about their intellectual capacity nor talk down to them as if they were children.

An informative task is to tape-record the speech of someone with cerebral palsy and then play it back first at the recording speed then at a faster speed. When played back at normal speed, the speech will be slow and hard to understand but in many cases it will sound almost the same as a normal speaker when played back faster.

It is apparent that as an interviewer one will need to be prepared to listen carefully and wait for the answer to be completed. Do not rush in to repeat or correct but be prepared to wait until the response is completed. As the effort of speaking is also accompanied by other uncontrolled motor behaviour the interviewer must concentrate on the words, not on the non-verbal behaviour which will not be similar to that of a normal speaker.

The use of computers and computer-aided recording devices can be of great assistance. Training is required but there are many advantages. The interviewer can present the questions both orally and on the screen and the respondents can type in their answers at their own pace. Probing can be carried out by moving the contents of the screen to the desired place and back. A permanent record is created as both questions and answers are recorded as the interview proceeds.

Hearing disability

Hearing disability can include a range of impairment from mild to severe. In addition, there may be partial impairment in one ear only or impairment in specific frequencies (for example, high-frequency deafness). Causes include faulty development of the aural system, onset as a result of an infection such as meningitis, and the effects of exposure to noise such as to loud music or industrial noise. As already noted, loss of hearing acuity is common in the elderly.

The degree of disability will determine the most appropriate ways of conducting the interview. When minor or partial impairment is suspected, a preliminary check can be made to obtain optimum voice level and for the interiewer to arrange to sit on the respondent's best side for hearing.

With more severe degrees of deafness, different techniques are needed. Those who regularly work with the deaf may use sign language and lipreading but an interviewer who is not constantly in contact with the hearing impaired is unlikely to have developed these skills. The use of a computer-aided display is one way this problem can be overcome. A computer such as a laptop has the added advantage that it can be taken to the respondent's location. The visual display allows the respondent to respond verbally or type in the answers as the questions appear on the display screen. The method can be interactive, with the interviewer and respondent both involved. Non-verbal communication can be added as additional cues. The method may require some preliminary training if the respondent is not familiar with using a computer.

Deafness is not related to any particular degree of intellectual functioning. The most likely problems to arise are those related to social skills.

To maximise contact with a less severely impaired respondent, speak clearly but do not shout into a hearing aid. Keep your face in clear view so that they can respond to non-verbal cues and make use of lipreading. Do not slow your natural pace of speaking and do not exaggerate speech sounds. Hearing aids magnify all sounds, not only the interviewer's voice, so a quiet environment is very important. Keep your own background noise at a minimum so that the respondent is not distracted.

Visual impairment

As with hearing loss, there are varying degrees of visual impairment. Some people are congenitally blind, but visual impairment can also arise from infections such as trachoma, from injury, from diseases such as diabetes and from degenerative conditions (such as cataracts). Whereas the incidence of severe impairment is low (about 2 per cent of the population), the occurrence of developmental degenerative cataracts in the elderly has been reported as being around 80 per cent (Gething, Healy, Cutler, Geniale, Lean-Fore & Walker, 1984). Trachoma is most prevalent in Aboriginal groups in the outback. Recent improvements in eye surgery have brought about an increase in the number of successful treatments of trachoma and cataracts.

The different types of impairment lead to different methods of interviewing. In the case of congenital impairment the child has had to learn to process all information using other senses, whereas in the case of acquired impairment the person can rely on memories but has to learn new ways of processing. It does not follow automatically that the blind are compensated by greater acuity in other senses: this acuity has to be learned. There is no relationship between the degree of visual impairment and intelligence, and the whole range of intellectual ability is present among the visually impaired.

Interviewing techniques which rely strongly on verbal communication are appropriate, but the interviewer has to remember that the expression of feelings and reactions by non-verbal gestures must be omitted. Pitch of voice will provide further information.

In opening the interview the interviewer should state his or her name clearly and give clear verbal messages in regard to credentials. If there is written documentary support, the details should be read out. If the respondent's vision is severely impaired either a Braille text can be used or a tape-recording of the person confirming authorisation and credentials. Deteriorating acuity and cataracts in the elderly are not usually so severe as to require either of these methods of presenting credentials. However, large, clear type should be used for any written materials.

Intellectual impairment

There are many types of intellectual impairment. Here we will consider interviewing with respondents who have mild to moderate disability. One of the best-known sources of such disabilities is Down's syndrome.

A respondent with intellectual disability has difficulty in comprehending complex sentences, in remembering and in reading and may have a speech and language problem—problems that can occur to different degrees in individuals. Such a person has the same needs and desires for social and sexual behaviour as any normally functioning respondent would; indeed, the need of intellectually disabled people for acceptance may be even greater than that of the normal respondent because they have been rejected by others so often.

The wording of questions needs to be precise and plain. Avoid complex grammatical constructions, the hypothetical, subjunctives, irony, rhetorical questions. (This is, in any case, good practice for all interviewing.) Of course, the conceptual level of the questions must be adapted to suit the skills of the respondent. Treat one idea at a time, but do not talk down. Be prepared to wait while a response is thought through. Above all, show respect and acceptance of your respondent as an individual and do not treat an adult as a child.

Multiple disabilities

Although it is important not to make judgements about intellectual functioning on the basis of physical and sensory disabilities of the types discussed above, it is nevertheless possible that you may have to interview respondents who have a combination of disabilities. Some persons with physical or sensory disabilities may also have some intellectual disability while the conceptual abilities of others may be masked by their difficulties in hearing, vision and language production.

It does not follow that each of the contributing disabilities will have equal severity or equal influence upon communication in an interview. In the case of respondents with spina bifida, for example, spinal chord lesion is combined with cortical impairment. This presents as physical disability combined with some intellectual impairment, but differences in individuals and in the location of the brain injury create an unevenness in development.

Moderate degrees of combined hearing and vision impairment present a problem of organisation to maximise the respondent's understanding of the questions, but cases of severe disability are not suitable for interviewers who do not work in this field.

SUMMARY

This chapter can only introduce students to some of the issues they will encounter when conducting interviews with people with disabilities. There is a vast literature on this subject and those who plan to work in this field will need other more advanced skills than have been suggested here.

What has been emphasised is that there is a great range of individual differences and degrees of severity. All people with disabilities want to be accepted for themselves as they are; the interviewer must put the person first, not the disability. Adults are not children, and disabilities, whether physical or intellectual, do not make them so. In whatever way possible, it is important to concentrate on making use of the skills the respondents have rather than on their disability.

Managing time will require more care than with other interviews. Where speech is impaired it does not mean that the question was not understood. You may have to allow for longer interviews so that a respondent who takes longer to formulate replies does not feel pressured.

It was also indicated that there are now many ancillary methods which can be introduced, such as modern computer aided devices.

ACTIVITIES FOR STUDENTS

Are there students on your campus who have any of the disabilities discussed in this chapter? Find a way to meet with some of them.

If possible, ask a person with a disability to meet with your class and talk about what it is like to live with that disability. See *Living with Disabilities* (Gething, Healy, Cutler, Geniale, Lean-Fore & Walker, 1984) for some personal accounts.

What was your first reaction to this person? Did it change after you got to know him or her better?

Only when you feel comfortable with meeting other such people, begin to plan your interview schedule. Set up the questions in the usual way but so that they can be presented in ways that maximise abilities your respondents have.

If you have a laptop or access to a computer you might like to try your hand at developing a program to present your questions and have your respondent answer this way.

To begin with, choose a topic which is not too threatening but will be worth discussing.

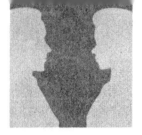

chapter

13

INTERVIEWING
ACROSS CULTURES

The use of interviewing in cross-cultural research, which was discussed in chapter 7, is a relatively uncommon application compared with the many other situations in which interviews are conducted with people of differing cultural backgrounds. In this chapter we will consider some of the demands which these situations place upon interviewers and respondents.

In multicultural Australia today, as in other multicultural countries, it is almost impossible for professional workers not to have some contact with clients and co-workers or members of the general public who come from a cultural background different from their own. Both culture and language may differ. In the tourism and travel industry, in over-the-counter services and in the health service fields, dealing with people of non-English speaking background is an everyday occurrence. How can we make such interviews most effective?

Cultural factors affect the relationship between interviewer and respondent, the respondent's motivation and understanding of the content of the interview, the choice of appropriate language and non verbal communication. The recognition of cultural norms which might differ from those of one's own culture marks the beginning of mutual understanding, without which the interviewer will experience a degree of frustration.

The criteria for good interviewing which were set down in earlier chapters also apply to interviewing across cultures but there are also other aspects unique to this type of interview. For example, if you do not speak the respondent's language an interpreter may need to be called in. What is the most appropriate way to use that interpreter? Are there age or generation differences within immigrant groups which differ from age or generation differences within the host society and therefore call for different approaches? In organisations what differences could there be with job interviews when applicants come from different cultural backgrounds?

Communication issues

Research on cross-cultural communication (Gallois & Callan, 1997; Brislin, 1986; Cushner & Brislin, 1996) has examined communication issues in many contexts. When the language of the interviewer differs from that of the respondent some problems of syntax, vocabulary and register arise. However, communication problems also arise when the language is the same but cultural norms differ. This occurs in non-verbal communication and in interpreting underlying meaning and intention. Both language and cultural norm differences can occur together.

When we interview people from ethnic minorities within Australia, the level of their English proficiency will be an important factor. Difficulty with the English language is most likely to be experienced by elderly first-generation immigrants, particularly older women whose migration has been sponsored under family reunion programs and those from remote villages in countries where English is not spoken widely. Two such groups are those from Iran and Greece.

Among younger family members who have lived most of their lives in Australia knowledge of English is not such a problem. Because of generational changes, however, younger family members may experience some conflict between traditional values and those of their Australian peers (see chapter 10), which can affect the relationship between interviewer and respondent.

Using interpreters

When should you use an interpreter and who should interpret? Although there are official interpreter services many people do not make use of them. The reasons vary, but the services may not be readily available in all situations, such as in smaller country towns.

Because the children have greater facility in English than their parents, they have been used as interpreters in government services interviews, in interviews with representatives of banking and other commercial organisations, in schools, and by doctors and others in the health professions. However, to have to rely on the child can mean a serious loss of status for the parent. Also, in the course of the interview, information may be asked for which the parent does not want to provide in the presence of the child. Another problem is the burden the demand can place upon their children to make themselves available: the younger children will usually need to leave their schooling; the older children will need to leave their employment or other caring commitments.

Care should be taken to select an interpreter who is culturally acceptable as well as proficient in the language. Where there is conflict between ethnic groups either in the host country or in their country of origin, knowledge of the language is not a sufficient criterion. The conflict could be political as in the case of the former Yugoslavia, but there political differences are also linked to religious differences between Muslims and Christians. Schisms between differing branches of a church, as in the case of the Macedonian and the Greek branches of the Eastern Orthodox Church, make it difficult for an interpreter from the opposite side even if that person's ability in the language is unquestionable. It is less a question of whether the interviewer is tolerant or not than the degree of acceptance by the respondent and the respondent's community.

The role of the interpreter is to assist the interviewer and respondent, not to take over the respondent or interviewer's role. Do not allow the interpreter to intrude his or her own views, or give their own construction to the respondent's feelings and intentions. Questions should always be addressed to the respondent, not the interpreter. Where possible, place the interpreter a little behind the line of sight between interviewer and respondent.

CULTURAL DIFFERENCES

Cultural differences in politeness norms

When interviewing within one's own culture, we need to be aware of, and adhere to the politeness norms of our own society. Equally, when interviewing a person from a different culture, we would want to observe the politeness norms of that culture. Sometimes, however, these encounters do not go as we would have expected and we feel uncomfortable that our good intentions do not appear to be reciprocated. It might appear, too, that the other person is also a little bewildered and embarrassed.

In general, the more the interviewer can learn about the culture of the respondent, the less likely it is there will be a failure to meet the cultural expectations. There are also many individual differences in the degree of tolerance for social ineptitude. The respondents' experience of people from outside their own culture, their education and social position in their own culture and their degree of embeddedness within the culture will affect their attitudes to others' behaviour.

To illustrate how some simple differences can occur, consider the following three examples. They are drawn from conversational interludes rather than from formal interviews but each involves asking questions.

In China a middle-aged lady, Mrs Brown, and her husband are being entertained at a rather lavish dinner by senior members of the company to which Mr Brown is attached in the Australian branch. Mrs Brown is taken aback when the first question put to her is, 'How old are you?'. She mumbles a vague reply, privately thinking how rude it is to ask a woman her age, especially when she would rather give the impression of being somewhat younger than she is. She does not realise that she is being shown respect for her advanced years.

The situation then worsens. Her Chinese host follows this up with, 'How much money does your husband earn?'. She has difficulty in deciding how to react: should she tell him exactly how much or should she try to avoid answering. She regards this as a rude question. If her host really wanted to know how much, he surely could find out, but this is to her not a topic for the dinner table. She is also a little embarrassed because her husband's salary is so much more than that of her hosts, who, she thinks, can ill afford the luxury of the expensive dinner.

The host perceives her discomfiture and tries again with another question, 'How many children do you and Mr Brown have?'. As the Chinese naturally would expect a woman of Mrs Brown's age and position to have children and even grandchildren, this should have been easier. Mrs Brown cheerfully replies that she does not have any children by her present husband, although she has two, one from each of two former marriages. At this the conversation becomes a little subdued as divorces are neither common nor approved in China. Mrs Brown wonders why the atmosphere has changed.

The second example comes from Japan. In this case the Australian visitor, Edward Williamson (call me Ted, he insists), has been asking his Japanese friend probing questions about Japanese economic conditions and Japan's relations with other countries and Australia in particular. He reports how friendly and agreeable his host was, and how straightforward was his assessment of the situations they had discussed, although he says he 'couldn't take all that bowing'.

What Ted does not see at the time, nor realise later, is that the smiling appearance, the agreeableness and apparent openness are politeness behaviour which conceals his friend's true feelings. His Japanese friend is actually embarrassed to use the familiar name Ted as he does not consider they are on such a familiar basis; but he does it out of consideration for Ted. He is, in fact, feeling sorry for Ted's gaucheness and ignorance and is trying to cover up to help his Australian friend save face. Alternatively, he might completely disagree with all that the Australian is saying, holding him in contempt. Politeness forbids that he should reveal these feelings, so he presents a smiling face and conveys the appearance of an acceptance which he does not actually feel.

The third example is from Thailand. Perhaps no culture has developed a more sensitive code of politeness behaviour. Training of children emphasises being considerate for others and self-abasement (Suvannathat, 1985) and leads in the mature adult to relationships being expressed in sophisticated and elegant politeness behaviour stressing a consideration for others which is embedded in the importance of hierarchical relationships. When asking someone questions, it is therefore important to do so in ways which do not allow the other to feel inferior or wrong. Segaller (1993) and Klausner (1993) provide many insights into Thai culture.

The following incident was related to this writer by two Australians who had been travelling by landrover in Thailand and were trying to reach Chiang Mai. It seemed that they must be near but they saw no signs. They passed through a number of villages but found it was hard to communicate. Finally they found someone who spoke English. 'Is this the road to Chiang Mai?' they asked. 'Yes', was the reply. 'How far?' 'About twenty kilometers.' They thanked their informant and drove on. About twenty kilometers further on there was no sign of the city. They tried again. 'Is this the road to Chiang Mai?' 'Yes.' 'How far is it from here?' 'About forty kilometers.' They began to be concerned that surely they weren't that far out of their way. Certainly, they had not followed the main road, preferring to see more of the countryside. Some further questions finally put them right. Yes, this was the road to Chiang Mai, but they had been travelling in the opposite direction. Their informants had not wished to point out their mistake.

These three examples are taken from informal social encounters. How can we avoid making similar mistakes in the more constrained situation of an interview, where the posing of questions is the principal method of obtaining information? While there can be no simple set of rules to fit all cultures, nevertheless a few points may illustrate.

When interviewing a person of Muslim background, always use the right hand, especially for giving and taking food.

Thai Buddhists regard the head as sacred; do not pat a child on the head.

Eye contact is not regarded as polite in many cultures. It can be regarded as insolent in children. Many indigenous Australians and North Americans conduct conversations seated beside each other rather than seated opposite, avoiding direct eye contact.

Acceptable social distance varies greatly (See the work of Hall, 1966; Sommer, 1969; Proshansky, Ittelson & Rivlin, 1976).

Even though the interviewer is not familiar with the finer points of politeness norms in the culture of the respondent, attitudes will be most effective which emphasise consideration for others, recognising the possibility of making mistakes and being prepared to admit them to oneself. Remember that in all cultures there are great individual and social differences in politeness norms. Be prepared to accept that the response may not represent the underlying attitude. Watch for the non-verbal indicators of anxiety.

Names

Names give much information about a person's culture and status. It is well to become familiar with some of the ways in which the use of names varies across cultures so that errors are avoided in addressing respondents.

Chinese names can at first lead to some confusion, owing to the sequence of names. Confusion arises partly because some Chinese people change the sequence of their names to accommodate Western practices and partly because this different order is used to enter their names in class rolls and registers. The proper order is family name, followed by generation name (which is the same for all brothers, sisters and cousins of the same generation) and, lastly, individual given name. So, Wong Fei Gang should appear under W, not G in any alphabetical listing, and be addressed by his family name. When Chinese people also have adopted a Christian name, this name is added in, sometimes before the family name and sometimes last, after the given names. Some people now do not include the generation name and have only the given name; the generation name is often linked to the given name, by a hyphen or by running the two names into a single word.

Muslim names also cause confusion to those not familiar with them. They are made up of the given name followed by 'bin' or 'binte' (to indicate whether the son of, or daughter of), then the father's name. This pattern becomes more complex when an extra given name is included and when the person or the father has been on the haj (the pilgrimage to Mecca). Hereditary and awarded titles precede the names of both the person and, if relevant, the father. So, a Malay Muslim man can be called Wan Haji Mohammed Rahim bin Wan Haji Abdul Rizal. The first word is not a name but a hereditary title; the name by which to address the person is Rahim and in formal speech this is preceded by Wan Haji. To make it easier for Western use the father's name may sometimes be treated as a surname, but this is not strictly correct. For a woman the same sequence applies. She does not take her husband's name on marriage.

These are but two examples from two of the largest groups whose naming practices differ from English-based/Western ones. Other groups with different naming traditions are the Sikhs, Thais, and Spaniards. Indian names also reveal religion, region and caste. It is very useful to be aware of what the person's name conveys.

Dress

As with names, dress can tell you much about the cultural background but beware of making superficial judgements. For example, both Hindu and Muslim women from the Indian subcontinent wear saris. However, the Hindu woman may be distinguishable from the Muslim woman by the caste mark on her forehead, while the Muslim woman may wear the burkha (which covers her dress completely). When a woman wears a burkha, her social background is not apparent. Do not judge intelligence or education by the amount of covering worn.

Cultural differences in gender roles affecting interviewing

This issue has been touched on above in relation to the use of children as interpreters as it is most often the mother who has to use her child in this capacity. In research the issue relates to using interviewers of the same gender. However, the question can be important also in interviews with health professionals, and in social security and family welfare contexts.

In traditional Muslim communities such as among the Lebanese and Iraqi ethnic migrant groups, it would be difficult for a woman to be interviewed without her husband being present, and quite impossible for a woman to be interviewed by a man. As head of the family, the husband may also insist on vetting the questions and responding on his wife's behalf. Whether his interpretation is consistent with that of his wife or not, she may be unable to contradict him, at least not to an outsider.

Empathy is needed to try to see the situation from a different cultural perspective. The norms of gender role expectations which, like all cultural norms, are taken for granted and acted upon without question are learned, first acquired in childhood and later internalised in the value system (Keats, 1982; 1986). Migrants to another country have to acquire a new set of behavioural norms which often may conflict with those of their original cultural background. An interesting finding, however, is that the norms and values may change more in the home country than in the migrant communities in their new home. (Georgas, 1989)

SUMMARY

In this chapter some differences between interviewing respondents from one's own culture and those from a different background have been shown. The problems in using an interpreter were raised. Communication issues in language, and cultural differences in politeness norms were discussed. Names and dress give useful clues to cultural background and some examples of non-Western styles were given.

Although differences were stressed, the importance of treating each respondent as an individual cannot be overstated. Cultures are not static and there are as many variations within cultures as between them. The differences make for a challenge to interviewers but can make interviewing a person from a culture different from one's own a stimulating experience.

ACTIVITIES FOR STUDENTS

It should not be too difficult in a university or any large organisation to find some other student of a different cultural background to your own. Begin by talking informally about that person's first-hand experiences of cross-cultural differences; then on the basis of your information, make out a brief interview schedule. For each of the aspects discussed above include at least one question.

Afterwards, play back the tape and ask yourself what were your greatest problems of communication. Did you learn something new about the culture of that person?

Repeat the interview with people from different backgrounds until you have covered a range of cultures.

Discuss your experiences with your class group and fellow students.

chapter

14

SOME DIFFICULT CASES

No matter how careful you are about setting up your interview and no matter how hard you try to do all the right things to establish good rapport with your respondent, there will always be someone who is difficult to interview. Do not be too quick to blame yourself but try to recognise the nature of the problem. In this chapter some of the ways in which respondents are difficult to deal with are discussed, together with some strategies to help you understand the source of the problems and reduce anxiety levels in both respondent and interviewer.

Here we are not considering the kind of communication difficulties which are found with people with disabilities, or with aged respondents or people from another culture. Nor will this chapter add further to the cultural issues raised in chapter 13. What we are considering here are emotional responses, attitudes and behaviour which can inhibit mutual cooperation and affect interpersonal relationships between interviewer and respondent in any interview situation. They can occur regardless of cross-cultural factors. Hostility and anxiety, and prejudicial attitudes to an interviewer's gender, age and status are not uncommon problems. Difficulties are also posed for the interviewer by respondents who give thoughtless answers, by those who agree politely with everything the interviewer says even though their private opinions differ, and by those who are verbose and find it hard to keep to the point. These difficult cases can occur in any interview type and are not uncommon.

Because the interviewer–respondent relationship is a dynamic one, difficult behaviour by the respondent can trigger a reaction by the interviewer. We need to guard against adopting the same attitudes as the respondent. Hostility must not be allowed to arouse more hostility, nor must anxieties be escalated.

The hostile respondent

Hostility from a respondent is the most common problem recognised by interviewers. It can be overt or covert in expression. The language used is the most obvious way in which it manifests itself, but non-verbal messages can also convey hostility, both overtly and covertly by body posture, gestures and facial expressions (chapter 6 looks at interpreting non-verbal messages). Such hostility can be directed towards the topic of the interview and/or the interviewer.

Hostility to the topic can arise when the theme of the interview touches some feeling which is unacceptable. For example, it might be that the topic is highly challenging, such as a topic with a sexual theme, in which case both anger at being questioned and anxiety about revealing one's attitudes or behaviour may both be involved.

Another possible source of hostility to the topic is when the person really feels anger about the matter under discussion. An example of this might be in an interview about crime and drug dependency, when the respondent has strong feelings against people involved in those activities.

The timing of the interview may be enough to arouse hostility if it is inconvenient and other activities of more interest to the respondent have been put aside to do the interview. This would be especially likely to occur if the respondent has agreed to the interview only after having been pressured to participate and feels resentful because of having acquiesced. There could also be other demands upon the person's time and the interview is preventing the respondent from carrying out these tasks. Typical examples of this would be when the respondent has little time available at work, or when the mother of a young baby knows that the child will soon wake and need attention.

Although the respondent has unfavourable feelings about the topic, or the content of the questions, the hostility may be directed towards the interviewer rather than the content of the interview. This could occur in each of the examples above. Another situation is when the respondent has had a poor experience with a previous interview and carries over the antagonistic feelings to another interviewer. Another case is when the respondent is prejudiced against the interviewer on personal grounds, as discussed below.

How can the interviewer handle hostile respondents?

- Recognise the signs, both verbal and non-verbal.
- Avoid soothing reassurances; try to find the cause through probing.
- Do not try to trivialise or minimise the hostility but accept the respondent's feelings as valid.
- Do not promise help to alleviate or change the condition which has aroused the hostility if you cannot in fact do so.
- Prepare the interview schedule and the appointment carefully so that the time is available and urgent matters and distractions will be avoided.
- Use cognitive restructuring to help the respondent look at the issue in different ways.
- Place the emphasis on verifiable facts and actions and ask questions on these first.
- Allow the respondent to express feelings later.
- Above all, do not return hostility with hostility.

The anxious respondent

Many signs of a high level of anxiety are to be seen in a respondent's behaviour. A highly anxious respondent may give confused answers, begin a sentence only to break off before completing it, forget what was said, hear questions partially or incorrectly, hesitate before responding and change the response before completing the answer. Some may not answer a question at all. Others become over-excited, and cannot stop talking. Others express their anxiety in bluster. Yet others who are unsure of themselves may express their own anxieties through hostility to the questions or to the interviewer.

Causes of anxiety can lie in the respondent's feelings about the topic under discussion, covering a wide range from guilt, fear and shame to lack of knowledge and inability to understand the concepts. Many people who have no experience with recording their ideas on tape-recorder or seeing themselves on videotape have high initial levels of anxiety at the beginning of an interview. A general low level of self-esteem and poor self-concept are also at the heart of some anxiety.

How can the interviewer help to reduce the respondent's anxiety levels?

- Take time to develop rapport.
- Make the purpose of the interview clear so that irrelevant sources of anxiety are removed.
- Give plenty of practice with the tape-recorder or video recording.

- Begin with the least-threatening questions.
- Provide a calm, quiet environment, free of distractions.
- Leave something on the table for the respondent to fiddle with. Many clinicians have a soft rubber ball to squeeze.
- Do not rush the respondent when responses are hesitant or confused.
- Keep calm; do not become flustered yourself.

Prejudice

As we noted in chapter 8, interviewing panels make many judgements about job applicants on the basis of first impressions. Respondents also make such judgements about the interviewer, and some of these judgements may be prejudiced. The respondent may have disapproved at the outset of the interviewer's age, gender, appearance or ethnic background.

Consider the following situations.

Suppose you are a young female student assigned to interview a middle-aged man whose political and social attitudes are known to be extremely rigid. He refuses to be interviewed by a 'chit of a girl'.

Suppose you are a young man of ethnic minority background in which your religion, dress and skin colour proclaim your different background from that of your older female respondent. You set up the appointment for the interview by telephone but at your first meeting the respondent draws back and is reluctant to carry out the interview.

Yet another student comes to conduct an interview in his usual dress of t-shirt with a lurid provocative decoration, earrings, casual footwear, and haircut which can only be described as unusual. The intended respondent is clearly uncomfortable at such a sight and immediately makes up his mind that this is a typical example of irresponsible youth.

What can the interviewer do in such situations to overcome the respondent's prejudiced attitudes and develop an effective relationship?

You cannot change your age, gender or ethnic background. But you can reduce the shock of an appearance which may be acceptable in your own environment but which does not consider its effect upon those from a different social background, whether more or less conservative or conventional than your own.

Avoid extremes in dress style and personal appearance. Adopting a dress style which tends toward the conservative is usually better than an unusual style which will distract the respondent from the content of the interview.

Do not try to overcome age-related prejudice by behaving in an older or younger manner or wear clothes which are meant for an older or younger person.

Prejudicial first impressions can be reduced by showing your own efficiency. Do not pretend to have more experience than you actually have.

State your credentials precisely but do not claim more qualifications than you actually possess in order to create a better impression. Carry out your own task well and as the interview proceeds the respondent's attitude may change to one that is more favourable.

Put the emphasis on the content and purpose of the interview rather on personal relationships.

Acquiescence

You may meet with some respondents who seem at first to be very easy to interview. They agree with almost everything you say. Although some appear timid, most are very pleasant in manner and clearly want to be helpful. It only occurs to you after the interview is well-advanced that this agreeableness seems a little false, that their agreement might be merely superficial. Perhaps their acquiescence arises out of politeness, but it might also be a facade to hide their private thoughts and feelings, which are contrary to what they are saying. We noted the importance of politeness norms in chapter 13. Could this be a culturally related behavioural style? Or is this a person with a blinkered view on the world, one who always avoids the unpleasant?

How can you test this out? How can you reach their true feelings?

Such people have a strong need for positive feedback. You will need to show your support and trust to encourage them to respond more thoughtfully.

Probing is the means to obtain more depth in the replies. Use the structures with feedback loops to return to the main themes.

Do not confront them with allegations which suggest that they are deliberately lying, but probe for retrospective clarification and/or elaboration.

Status differences

At times a junior member of an interviewing team may be assigned to interview a very senior person in an organisation, or a student may plan to include a high-status person in a research project. Many an inexperienced interviewer will be apprehensive about conducting such an interview. Will the high-status person be willing to be interviewed? Will you be treated with condescension or cooperation? How should you approach such an interview?

Time is probably important, so do not waste it by spending a long time overcoming your own nervousness with irrelevancies.

When making the appointment do not underestimate the time your interview will take. If you have not finished in the allotted time your interview may be abruptly terminated.

Use your credentials to establish your expertise and integrity. State them precisely when making the appointment and be prepared to have the supporting documents ready to present.

Do not inflate your own status in order to impress.

Put the emphasis on the content. If you have chosen such a person for interview it should have been because that person has something valuable to contribute to the topic. To show that you appreciate that contribution will best be done by concentrating on the topic rather than on your own feelings.

You will usually find that a job being done well is soon recognised by people who do their own jobs well and cooperation will follow.

SUMMARY

In this chapter we dealt with the problems of coping with hostile, anxious, and prejudiced respondents, and the difficulties for interviewers when having to interview people whose status differs from that of the interviewer. Patience and empathy with the anxious, and overcoming hostility with efficiency were suggested as effective strategies for all these difficult respondents. It was noted that hostility is frequently a way of expressing anxiety and low self-confidence.

Integrity in stating one's credentials and using time efficiently are helpful with high-status respondents.

ACTIVITIES FOR THE STUDENT

You can learn much about how you will manage these difficult cases by practising with a little role-playing.

For each of the cases discussed above, prepare some questions and practise taking the roles of interviewer and respondent, recording the outcome on video and audio tape. Try to have a turn in both roles so that you experience both sides of the relationship. Remember that the respondent has no responsibility to answer all your questions or to answer truthfully.

You can make the situations more realistic with some props. For example, some furniture to suit the high-status person can be arranged either to increase or decrease the social distance between interviewer and respondent.

Play back each episode and critically evaluate both the interviewer's and the respondent's behaviour.

The following questions apply specifically to a role-play involving a hostile respondent but can apply to each of the cases.

Did the interviewer keep to the schedule?

How did the interviewer feel as the target of the respondent's hostility? How did the respondent feel when giving hostile replies?

What non-verbal expressions of hostility were observed? Did the non-verbal behaviour convey the same messages as the verbal behaviour? Consider this question in relation to both the interviewer and the respondent.

As an interviewer, did you feel you were being influenced by the respondent's behaviour? In what ways?

The more you can practise these roles, the more you will be able to understand the point of view of others unlike yourself. Your aim as an interviewer is to achieve empathy rather than merely to control an emotional reaction.

chapter

15

INTERVIEWING IN SITUATIONS OF STRESS

T his chapter deals with interviewing in situations in which the respondent has either undergone some stressful experience or is in a situation which is emotionally stressful. The situation may be a sudden traumatic event, such as being involved in a road accident; or it may be a long-term state of high emotional arousal and fear as in situations of sustained domestic violence and child abuse. Other such situations include interviewing after community disasters such as floods and bushfires, eyewitnessing a crime or being the victim of a criminal assault. We will pay special attention to interviewing children by police and in the court.

The emphasis here is on gathering reliable information from the respondent rather than on the longer-term interviewing which is found in counselling and clinical therapeutic relationships.

The behaviour of people in stressful situations is often characterised by memory loss and cognitive disorganisation. Accounts of an accident may not be cohesive but fragmented. The person may vividly recall a small but trivial visual image, like a handbag with contents spilling on the pavement or a doll's arm half-hanging from its body, but be unable to give a temporally precise account of what happened. Perceptual failures distorting space and time are not uncommon.

When the event is seen as a community disaster out of the individual's control, a sense of comradeship can develop which helps to decrease the level of stress. However, if the assault is perceived as directed at the individual or at one's own group, stress levels will be higher.

Reliability of eyewitnesses

One of the greatest problems in interviews with witnesses of traumatic incidents, including crimes, is that of the accuracy of eyewitness accounts. Eyewitness evidence is easily manipulated by biased questioning but is also affected by the unreliability of the witnesses' identification of the person. Eyewitness accounts are particularly unreliable when the people involved are of a different racial background to that of the witness. Research in the United States by Malpass (Malpass, 1996) on the cross-race effect in eyewitness identification has shown that people are more able to identify correctly people of their own race. These results have been found to be stable and substantial over many experiments and many race combinations. Malpass (1996) reports that in a standard face-recognition experiment there is a false recognition rate of about 15 per cent for other-race faces. The implications for forensic interviewing after stressful situations such as assaults, accidents or criminal actions are evident.

Children as witnesses

The effectiveness of interviews with children as witnesses in court situations has been the focus of much research (Dent & Flin [eds], 1992). The evidence suggests that children who are questioned about their experiences of being sexually abused or ill-treated by adults, who are often family members, are in a highly stressful situation. The questions we must consider are what kinds of interview should be used and how reliable are children's responses to their questioners.

For a long time in British and United States courts children were not regarded as being able to give evidence truthfully or reliably (Flin, Bull, Boon & Knox, 1992). The consequence was that in many child abuse cases the child was never consulted (Steller & Boychuk, 1992). However, results of many studies now indicate that children can give reliable accounts. For example, experimental studies carried out by Luus & Wells (1992) found that, as eyewitnesses, eight-year-old children were as reliable as adults. However, there was a difference between direct examination and cross-examination. The children were as accurate in their recall of events as the adults under direct examination, but made more errors under cross-examination. Cross-examination presented more problems for the eight-year-olds than for the twelve-year-olds or the adults.

Statement validity analysis

Statement validity analysis (SVA) is a method of assessing sexual abuse complaints by collecting and systematically analysing information from interviews and other relevant factors in the case. Steller & Boychuk (1992, p.49) state that SVA is a diagnostic overall procedure which includes:

> (a) careful review of relevant case information, (b) preserved semi-structured interview of the child, (c) criteria based content analysis of the transcribed interview, (d) validity checks of additional case information, and (e) a systematic summarisation of content analysis and validity checks.

Of particular interest in the present context is the semi-structured interview. The inclusion of this type of interview was based on the recognition that free recall is likely to produce the greatest accuracy and volume of information from the child. The questions move from broad to specific and back as required. Open-ended questions are used to elicit the free recall and cue questions are used to obtain specifics such as locations.

Criteria-based content analysis

Criteria-based content analysis (CBCA), which was mentioned above, is applied to the verbatim transcript of a recorded interview with the child. Five major categories of criteria are identified and ratings are applied to each criterion—nineteen in all. The criteria are whether an actually experienced event is mentioned. Absence of the criteria does not necessarily indicate that the statement is false.

Steller & Boychuk define the five major categories as follows:

1 *General characteristics of the statement*
   This category includes three criteria: logical structure is present (that is, the statement as a whole makes sense); unstructured production; quantity of details.
2 *Specific contents*
   The four criteria in this category are: contextual embedding; descriptions of interactions; reproduction of conversation; unexpected complications during the incident.
3 *Peculiarities of content*
   The six criteria in this category are: unusual details; superfluous details; accurately reported details misunderstood; related external associations; accounts of subjective mental state; attribution of perpetrator's mental state.

4   *Motivation-related contents*
    The five criteria in this category are: spontaneous corrections; admitting lack of memory; raising doubts about one's own testimony; self-deprecation; pardoning the perpetrator.
5   *Offence-specific elements*
    This category contains one criterion only: details characteristic of the offence.

Steller & Boychuk (1992) examined the effectiveness of using CBCA and found a high degree of validity over a large number of interviews.

The system has been set out in some detail here because it would appear to have usefulness in interviews with children involved in criminal cases other than sexual abuse. It could also be used with adults as well as with children.

The cognitive interview

Like SVA and CBCA, the cognitive interview is used for recall of events, and is particularly useful for recall of stressful events. It has been used successfully in the United States and Britain in police interviewing with both adults and children (Flin, Bull, Boon & Knox, 1992).

The cognitive interview was developed by Fisher & Geiselman (1992) in an attempt to improve eyewitness memory. The method is based on two principles drawn from the cognitive theory of memory: first, encoding specificity, which states that the retrieval process is most effective when it is most similar to the encoding process; and second, that memory is not a unitary representation but is made up of a complex array of many features.

From these two principles four sets of instructions were derived. In the original form of the interview these were the following (Köhnken, Milne, Memon & Bull, 1998):

1   Report everything you can about the event.
    Interviewees were encouraged to report everything even though it might seem trivial, or they could only partially recall it.
2   Recreate both the feelings and the surrounding context of the event.
3   Use a variety of temporal orders. Do not try to put everything in its exact sequence.
4   Take the perspective of someone else present at the event.

It was found, in practice, with police interviewing that the original form did not meet all the problems of their investigations; as well, much information was not elicited. A so-called 'enhanced' form was therefore developed, which included more features, including rapport building, transferring control of the interview to the interviewee, non-verbal behaviour, appropriate uses of pauses and the relative effectiveness of different types of questions (Köhnken, Milne, Memon & Bull, 1998).

To examine the relative effectiveness of the original and the enhanced forms, Köhnken, Milne, Memon & Bull carried out a meta analysis of 42 studies with 55 individual comparisons involving 2500 interviews. The cognitive interviews were compared with a control group of structured interviews. Compared with the control group, the cognitive interviews showed a significant effect size for correctly recalled details and an increase in effect size for incorrect details. The effect size for incorrect details was greater for adults than children, and the enhanced version of the cognitive interview produced more errors than the original version.

Videotaping of children as witnesses

Videotaping of child witnesses is now an accepted procedure in Australian courts and has been shown to reduce the stress of children giving testimony (Cashmore, 1990). There are two ways in which a videotaped interview is used. The child may be interviewed outside the court using the video and the tape of the interview then presented as evidence without the child being required to attend. Alternatively, the child may be interviewed as part of the court proceedings. In this case the examination is part of the court testimony and is subject to cross-examination. These interviews have been conducted in another room with the child present and have also been carried out with the child in a distant location.

The evidence suggests that this is a very effective situation for many young children, especially as it may save them the difficulties of confronting the accused in the courtroom.

Critical incident stress de-briefing

Both survivors and witnesses of traumatic events such as road accidents, earthquakes, criminal assault, and community disasters such as flood and bushfire can suffer severe post-traumatic stress. Obtaining information in these situations may be necessary for police, ambulance workers and emergency services workers. These workers themselves also suffer from the stress of the situation.

Stress de-briefing is now widely used after such traumatic events, for example by Raphael (1986) after the Guildford train disaster and after the Newcastle (New South Wales) earthquake (Waring, 1992; Kenardy, Webster, Lewin, Carr, Hazell & Carter, 1996).

As set out by Kenardy, Webster, Lewin, Carr, Hazell & Carter (1996), critical incident stress de-briefing involves four types of de-briefing: on or near the scene de-briefing; initial de-briefing; formal de-briefing and follow-up de-briefing. Formal de-briefing involves seven phases and is carried out by a qualified mental health professional twenty-four to forty-eight hours after the event.

Despite its use in many traumatic situations, Kenardy, Webster, Lewin, Carr, Hazell & Carter found there has been little systematic evaluation of its effectiveness. Their study of the aftermath of the Newcastle earthquake, the 'Quake Impact Study', followed up the post-trauma reactions and general mental health over a period of two years in helpers who had undergone de-briefing and those who had not. The result did not show an improved rate of recovery in those who were de-briefed, even when the level of exposure and helping-related stress were taken into account. They concluded that more rigorous research was needed before a final evaluation of de-briefing was possible.

As we are interested more here with obtaining information than with long-term counselling, the earlier stages of the de-briefing are most relevant. Waring (1992) sets out some of the key approaches in post-trauma interviewing. Patience is important. Do not expect the whole story to be told on first asking. A chronological review of events surrounding the traumatic event will help cognitive reconstruction. This is similar to the approach of the cognitive interview (see also Keats, 1993).

SUMMARY

The situations discussed in this chapter call for more advanced interviewing skills than situations we have treated in previous chapters. The stress of being a witness to a crime, giving evidence in court and being involved in traumatic events such as the Newcastle earthquake all affect the likelihood of obtaining reliable and accurate information. Methods for improving accuracy of recall described were the use of statement validity analysis with its sub-set, criteria-based content analysis, and the cognitive interview.

Although stress de-briefing is now a widely accepted practice after a traumatic event, research suggests that its efficacy is not clear. However, the principles of good interviewing which have been set out in previous chapters also apply to interviewing people suffering from stressful experiences.

ACTIVITIES FOR STUDENTS

Before attempting to apply any of the methods discussed above with people in actual stressful situations, where one more person asking questions will only add to their burdens, students should try out, and master, the methods in normal situations.

Use role play and simulation in practice sessions, with video feedback where possible.

chapter

16

OVERVIEW

Working through a book such as this which aims to help students learn the techniques of interviewing in research and professional practice is like travelling on a journey. We began with a rationale for the journey: why interview, and when. We then took a broader look at the landscape: at the many kinds of interview, with their various purposes and features.

The next stages of the journey asked something of the traveller. How would you relate to the people you will meet along the way and how would they relate to you? What are the best ways of asking the people you meet about their ways of viewing the world. You soon needed to work up some expertise in asking them questions, and then to understand the meaning of the replies you received. You might also want to make some sort of order out of all the information which comes to you, with a view to telling others who follow some of your findings and even, perhaps, some of the pitfalls you have met along the way.

Thus equipped, you could then cope with some of the many strangers you would meet. And, being an enterprising traveller, you will not have been satisfied with merely reading about what others have said, but will try out these experiences for yourself. Of these experiences—like all new travel experiences—some will entertain and some will enlighten, while others will raise more problems than you had ever expected. As you move on, your traveller's skills improve with each new place you visit and each new group of people you meet.

Interviewing is constantly providing new experiences because every respondent has a unique contribution to make. This book cannot of itself provide those experiences, but it can help to make your own experiences with interviewing more effective and enjoyable. Skilled interviewing is neither luck nor art but the efficient execution of a complex of interacting skills. Those are what you have been introduced to in the preceding chapters. In this concluding chapter you can now look back at the route you have taken to see how far you have travelled.

The book began with a brief introduction to what was involved in an interview, what it is and what it is not, neither a simple chat nor just a conversation but a controlled discourse composed of questions and responses. The differences between interviews and questionnaires and psychological tests and scales were outlined and their unique styles distinguished. Interviews could often be used to complement questionnaires and psychological tests and scales, adding more individual personal information. By allowing respondents to give reasons for their answers, questionnaire and test data can be greatly enhanced, and given greater depth. Moreover, in an interview the escape from answering a particular question or test item by omitting it or using the evasive middle category is not available.

The many kinds of situations in which interviews are conducted were then reviewed in chapter 2. Characteristics of the major types were summarised, showing the great variety in depth, number of persons involved and purposes served. In depth they range from the fairly superficial exchanges of over-the-counter information services to the in-depth interviewing of counselling, clinical work and forensic investigation. In regard to the number of people involved, they range from the one-to-one interviewer–respondent interaction to the panel with several interviewers and one respondent (as in the job selection interview), and the situation of one interviewer and many respondents (as in the interview with a group delegation).

In regard to the purposes served, two contrasting functions emerged: either to work towards changing attitudes or behaviour with a view to overcoming some problem, as in the case of clinical work and counselling, or to obtain information about the respondent's present attitudes and behaviour. In this book we have concentrated on those interviews which seek to obtain information only, although it was also recognised that the experience of participating in an interview can have its own effect upon subsequent behaviour. Attitudes can change as the person comes to see a situation in a new light.

Another way of categorising interviews is on the basis of who is seeking the interview. Is it the respondent who needs information from the interviewer or is the interviewer seeking the information from the respondent? The former is typified in the office and over-the-counter enquiries; the latter, by the research interview and the forensic examination. The answer to this question affects the interviewer–respondent relationship in a number of ways. However, in the dynamic development of an interview it is possible for the roles to become interchangeable. This effect can be seen in the structure shown in figure 5.3, with its channelling which allows the respondent to dictate the course of the questions. It might also occur as the result of probing, as in the structure of figure 5.5 (both figures in chapter 5).

Following this broad review, the next group of four chapters introduced students to the skills of interviewing. Chapter 3 dealt with work on the interviewer–respondent relationship, showing how to create and maintain good rapport and how to bring the interview to its conclusion leaving both interviewer and respondent with a sense of having achieved something worthwhile. The interaction of cognitive, social and affective factors was stressed, especially in distinguishing between sympathy and empathy, and the danger of allowing judgemental attitudes, both favourable and unfavourable, to bias the relationship. The final part of this chapter covered ethical considerations in the relationship, in the storing and use of records and the problems inherent in promises of confidentiality and anonymity.

The next task, which we took up in chapter 4, was to consider ways in which questions could be phrased in order to obtain the required information most effectively. With the many different contexts set out in chapter 2, many ways of framing questions could be used. In addition to the open-ended question we could create questions in a variety of formats, combining open-ended questions with multiple-choice and ranking and combining oral questions with written. General and specific questions could be used, varying their order as the situation demanded. The content and purpose of the interview would suggest the most appropriate types. Whatever format is chosen, it is important to phrase the questions without ambiguity, in language understandable to the respondent, and without bias.

Chapter 5 examined how individual questions contribute to the interview as a whole. Keeping in mind the three phases of the interview—the opening, the main body of questions and the closing—we showed the different functions of several types of structure. The simplest structure, with each question and its response unrelated to the next question (as shown in figure 5.1) has its place when gathering background data and obtaining factual records which do not require further elaboration. The move to the second type (shown in figure 5.2) linked responses and questions in a chain response leads to the next question, and so on. There are many situations where this loose structure is appropriate. It occurs where only one response is given to each question. However, in many interviews the respondent gives answers which have several aspects. In this case the interviewer needs much more skill. These types of structure were seen in figures 5.3, 5.4 and 5.5. If the interviewer fails to make use of all the information, as in figure 5.3, the interview is channelled into the selected route. Whether this occurs because of the interviewer's conscious intention, because of biased attitudes, or because of not being aware of the consequences, the effect is that this structure does not fully exploit the available information. We saw how this could be avoided in the structures shown in figures 5.4 and 5.5, which show the effects of probing and remembering what was said.

In chapter 6 the skills of interpreting responses were introduced. Here the various methods of probing were treated. We dealt further with the question of bias, this time stressing the responsibility of the interviewer in interpreting responses and in the interpersonal relationships with the respondent. Occurring at the same time as a verbal response, or instead of one, non-verbal messages also have to be interpreted. As the vehicle of expressing feelings, non-verbal messages can support and enhance a verbal response; but we saw how the interviewer also needs to be watchful for those non-verbal indicators which contradict the verbal message through gestures, facial expressions, body movements or tone of voice. Probing is needed to ascertain the underlying response. We could expect to find this behaviour when respondents are attempting to cover up their hostility or anxiety, as we saw in chapter 14, or in the situations of emotional stress such as described in chapter 15.

Having mastered the basic principles and developed your interviewing skills, the next step was to see how these could be applied in the demanding context of research. Although interviewing is used by many researchers in subsidiary ways (although they may not realise how often), here we were concerned with using interviews as data sources. We considered how to set up the research with several types of research design, some of these using interviews as the sole data source, others combining interviews with other data sources. The interview schedule had to be prepared with care: to ensure that the questions were relevant and free of bias. Pilot studies and reliability checks were needed, so that when the sample was finally obtained there would be very little attrition from subjects unable or unwilling to respond. The ethical issues discussed in chapter 3 were of particular relevance to obtaining participants and protecting the data obtained.

To prepare the data for analysis the responses have to be coded into manageable categories. Here we faced the problem of how to handle the great variety of responses which interviewing can produce. We had to take into account the theoretical range as well as the actual range of responses.

The theoretical range should account for all possible types of response, although in practice the actual data may not use the entire range. Once the coding categories are established and responses allocated accordingly, the analysis can go ahead as in any other research. Reliability of the allocation to categories will need to be tested using a number of judges, first in the pilot work and then with a sample of the full data set. Quantitative and qualitative methods can be combined in a multi-method approach to obtain greater insights.

Finally in chapter 7 we took up the special case of interviewing in cross-cultural research. So often the instruments such as psychological tests and scales which one might use within one's own cultural environment are either not available or are unsuitable for another cultural context. It would be very misleading merely to translate a test or scale into another language and expect it to behave in the same way as in the culture of origin. Not only would the factor structure be likely to differ, but individual scores might not be interpretable in the same way. A great amount of work is needed before such scales can be safely adopted in another culture. In these circumstances the use of interviewing has many advantages. The problems of translation and the functional equivalence of concepts can be overcome with careful preparation of the interview schedule. The problems of sampling remain but would be just as difficult if any other instrument were used. The qualitative data which can be obtained from reasons is a great advantage in explaining the role of cultural factors in whatever is being studied.

With chapter 8 we moved to a new approach. Until this point the issues, principles and skills development were not linked to a particular respondent type. In chapters 8–15 we saw how those general notions could be applied to a range of situations and respondents. In these chapters more references to research using interviewing with these groups of respondents have been included, and for each chapter there is a set of suggested activities for students to become more familiar with that type of respondent. Some of these activities can be carried out individually, while others can be part of a class group program. Chapter 15 looked at the importance of being aware of the effects of stress and the ways it could be handled in interviews. Hopefully this chapter will complement other aspects of students' professional training.

These chapters could only sample the wide range of interviewing in professional practice. Nevertheless, by working through them students can hone their skills in a variety of situations. Nor should the groups be seen in isolation. For example, people with disabilities include children, adolescents and older people, and people of differing cultural backgrounds also are interviewed in organisational settings, as shown by Gallois & Callan (1997). Any of these respondents could be hostile or anxious; stress can affect people of any age.

The applications of interviewing in professional practice and in research do differ to some extent, as was shown in chapter 7. However, any difference in depth or extent of questioning should not preclude the research interviewer from paying attention to the need to develop good rapport, to be unambiguous and unbiased, and to listen carefully and thoughtfully when interpreting the responses. Even the most ephemeral interaction will be improved if these basic demands of good interviewing are fulfilled. In the professional practice of psychologists, social workers and others in the caring professions they are essential requirements.

An important difference between interviewing in professional practice and research is the use to which the answers are to be put. In research the demands for structure become more rigorous, as each part of the interview has to be designed to serve a specific purpose and contribute to the interpretation of the data. When that interpretation must depend upon statistical analysis rather than on conceptual analysis only, the questions have to be expressed in ways which will lead to that type of treatment. Other than these demands, research interviews have the same requirements as interviews in daily professional practice. In either case, interviewing is a powerful tool, and should be employed with the highest ethical standards and respect for one's respondents.

This has been a book for students. Whatever path you choose in the future, whether it be in business management, service industries, tourism, the helping professions or research, the skills of interviewing are likely to be needed. They are worth developing for the ability they will give you to handle a range of interactions with people, but they will also widen your own horizons as you meet and come to understand people who are different from yourself. The journey once begun will take you much further yet.

REFERENCES

Aamodt, M.G. (1991) *Applied Industrial/Organizational Psychology*. Calif.: Brooks Cole.

Anastasi, A. & Urbina, S. (1997) *Psychological Testing*. N.J.: Prentice Hall. Seventh Edition.

Argyle, M. (1992) *The Social Psychology of Everyday Life*. London: Routledge.

Australia, Government of. Bureau of Statistics Demographic Report, December, 1998.

Australian Psychologist, (1999) *34*, (2) Special Issue . Psychology and the Older Person.

Avery, G. & Baker, E. (1990) *Psychology at Work*. Sydney: Prentice Hall. Second Edition.

Baltes, P.B. & Baltes, M.M. (Eds) (1990) *Successful Aging: Perspectives from Behavioral Sciences*. Cambridge: Cambridge University Press.

Brislin, R.W. (1986) The wording and translation of research instruments. In W.J. Lonner & J.W. Berry (Eds), *Field Methods in Cross-Cultural Research*. Beverly Hills, Calif: Sage. pp.137–164.

Brown, R. (1973), *A First Language*. Harmondsworth, Middlesex: Penguin.

Cashmore, J. (1990) The use of video technology for child witnesses. *Monash Law Review, 16*, 228–250.

Cushner, K. & Brislin, R. (1996) *Intercultural Interactions: A Practical Guide*. Thousand Oaks, Calif.: Sage.

Dent, H. (1992) The effect of age and intelligence on eyewitnessing ability. In H. Dent & R. Flin (Eds), *Children as Witnesses*. Chichester: Wiley. pp1–13.

Dent, H. & Flin, R. (Eds) (1992) *Children as Witnesses*. Chichester: Wiley.

Drever, P. (1998) Going ... going ... grey. *In-Psych, 20*, 5, 14–15.

Eckman, P. (Ed.) (1982) *Emotion in the Human Face*. Cambridge: Cambridge University Press. Second edition.

Eckman, P. & Friesen, W.V. (1975) *Unmasking the Face*. Englewood Cliffs, N.J.: Prentice Hall.

Feather, N.T. (1998) Attitudes toward high achievers, self-esteem, and value priorities for Australian, American and Canadian students. *Journal of Cross-Cultural Psychology, 29*, 749–759.

Fielding, N.G. & Lee, R.M. (Eds) (1991) *Using Computers in Qualitative Research*. London: Sage.

Fisher, R.P. & Geiselman, R.E. (1992) *Memory-Enhancing Techniques for Investigative Interviewing: The Cognitive Interview*. Springfield, Ill.: Charles Thomas.

Flin, R., Bull, R., Boon, J. & Knox, A. (1992) Children in the witness-box. In H. Dent & R. Flin (Eds), *Children as Witnesses*. Chichester: Wiley. pp.167–179.

Frydenberg, E. & Lewis, R. (1994) Coping with different concerns: Consistency and variation in coping strategies used by adolescents. *Australian Psychologist, 29*, 45–48.

Furnham, A. (1992) *Personality at Work; The Role of Individual Differences in the Workplace*. Routledge: London.

Gallois, C. & Callan, V. (1997) *Communication and Culture: A Guide for Practice*. Chichester: Wiley.

Georgas, J. (1989) Changing family values in Greece: From collectivist to individualist. *Journal of Cross-Cultural Psychology, 20*, 1, 80–91.

Gething, L. (1997) *Person to Person: A Guide for Professionals Working with People with Disabilities*. Sydney: Maclennan+Petty.

Gething, L., Healy, K., Cutler, S.G., Geniale, P., Lean-Fore, S. & Walker, E. (1984). *Living with Disabilities*. Sydney: Cumberland College of Health Sciences.

Ghuman, P.A.S. (1999) *Asian Adolescents in the West*. Leicester: B.P.S. Books.

Gibson, J.T., Westwood, M.J., Ishiyama, F.I., Borgen, W.A. et al. (1991) Youth and culture: A seventeen nation study of perceived problems and coping strategies. *International Journal for the Advancement of Counselling, 14*, 203–216.

Gorden, R.L. (1969) *Interviewing: Strategies, Techniques, and Tactics*. Homewood, Ill.: Dorsey Press.

Hall, E.T. (1966) *The Hidden Dimension*. New York: Doubleday.

Haslam, S.A., McGarty, C., Oakes, P. & Turner, J. (1993) Social comparative context and illusory correlation: Testing between ingroup bias and social identity models of stereotype formation. *Australian Journal of Psychology, 43*, 97–101.

Herriot, P. (1991) The selection interview. In P. Warr (Ed.), *Psychology at Work*. London: Penguin. Third Edition. pp.139–159.

Kafer, N.F. (1993) Non-verbal communication. In D. Keats, *Skilled Interviewing*. Melbourne: ACER. Second Edition. pp.69–78.

Keats, D.M. (1997) *Culture and the Child: A Guide for Professionals in Child Care and Development*. Chichester: Wiley.

Keats, D. [M.] (1993) *Skilled Interviewing*. Melbourne: ACER. Second Edition.

Keats, D.M. (1986) Using the cross-cultural method to study the development of values. *Australian Journal of Psychology, 38*, 297–308.

Keats, D.M. (1982) The development of values in Malaysian and Australian adolescents. In J.L.M. Binnie-Dawson, G.H. Blowers & R. Hoosain (Eds), *Perspectives in Asian Cross-Cultural Psychology: Selected Papers from the First Asian Regional Conference of the International Association for Cross-Cultural Psychology*. (pp.68–95) Lisse: Swets & Zeitlinger.

Keats, D.M. & Fang, F.-X. (1996) The development of concepts of fairness in rewards in Chinese and Australian children. In H. Grad, A. Blanco & J. Georgas (Eds), *Key Issues in Cross-Cultural Psychology*. (pp.276–287) Lisse: Swets & Zeitlinger.

Kenardy, J.A., Webster, R.A., Lewin, T.J., Carr, V.J., Hazell, P.L. & Carter, G.L. (1996) Stress debriefing and patterns of recovery following a natural disaster. *Journal of Traumatic Stress, 9*, 37–49.

King, N. (1994) The qualitative research interview. In C. Cassell & G. Symon (Eds), *Qualitative Methods in Organizational Research A Practical Guide*. London: Sage. pp.14–36.

Klausner, W.J. (1993) *Reflections on Thai Culture: Collected Writings of William J. Klausner*. Bangkok: The Siam Society.

REFERENCES

Kudci, D.A. & Ferguson, S.J. (1998), The status of geropsychology in Australia: Exploring why Australian psychologists are not working with elderly clients. *Australian Psychologist, 33*, 2, 96–100.
Köhnken, G., Milne, R., Memon, A. & Bull, R. (1998) The cognitive interview: A meta-analysis. *Psychology, Crime and Law.*
Kornadt, H.-J., Hayashi,T., Tachibana, Y., Trommsdorff, G., & Yamauchi, H. (1992) Aggressiveness and its developmental conditions in five cultures. In S. Iwawaki, & Y. Kashima (Eds), *Innovations in Cross-Cultural Psychology.* Amsterdam: Swets & Zeitlinger. pp.250–268.
Leonard, R. (1995), The interpretation of discrepancies in multimethod research: A comparison of children's negotations in two research contexts. *Early Development and Parenting, 4,* 21–28.
Leonard, R. & Burns, A. (1999) Turning points in the lives of midlife and older women. *Australian Psychologist, 34*, (2), 87–93.
Lupton, D. (1992), Discourse analysis: A new method for understanding the ideologies of health and illness. *Australian Journal of Public Health, 16*, 145–150.
Luszcz, M.A. (1992), Predictors of memory in young-old and old-old adults. *International Journal of Behavioral Development, 15*, 147–166.
Luszcz, M. & Hinton, M. (1995) Domain and task-specific beliefs about memory in adulthood: A microgenetic approach. *Australian Journal of Psychology, 47*, 54–59.
Luus, L. & Wells, G.L. (1992) The perceived credibility of child eyewitnesses. In H. Dent & R. Flin (Eds), *Children as Witnesses.* Chichester: Wiley. pp.73–92.
Malpass, R.S. (1996) Face recognition at the interface of psychology, law, and culture. In H. Grad, A. Blanco & J. Georgas (Eds), *Key Issues in Cross-Cultural Psychology.* Lisse: Swets & Zeitlinger. pp.7–21.
Memon, A. & Bull, R. (1999) *Handbook of the Psychology of Interviewing.* Chichester: Wiley.
Morris, R. (1994) Computerised content analysis in management research: A demonstration of advantages and limitations. *Journal of Management, 20*, 903–931.
Munroe, R.L. & Munroe, R.H. (1994) *Cross-Cultural Human Development.* Prospect Heights, Illinois: Waveland Press.
Potter, J. & Wetherall, M. (1987) *Discourse and Social Psychology: Beyond Attitudes and Behaviour.* London: Sage.
Proshansky, H.M., Ittelson, W.H. & Rivlin, L.G. (1976) *Environmental Psychology: People and Their Physical Settings.* New York, Holt, Rinehart & Winston. Second Edition.
Raphael, B. (1986) *When Disaster Strikes: How Individuals and Communities Cope with Catastrophe.* New York: Basic Books.
Ribeau, P. & Poppleton, S.E. (1978) *Psychology and Work: An Introduction.* London: Macmillan. Reprinted 1992.
Segall, M.H., Dasen, P.R., Berry, J.W. & Poortinga,Y.H. (Eds) (1990). *Human Behavior in Global Perspective: An Introduction to Cross-Cultural Psychology.* New York: Pergamon.
Segaller, D. (1993) *Thai Ways.* Bangkok: Post Books. Third Edition.
Selman, R.L. (1980) *The growth of Interpersonal Understanding.* New York: Academic Press.
Sommer, R. (1969) *Personal Space.* Englewood Cliffs, N.J.: Prentice Hall.
Statt, D.A. (1994) *Psychology and the World of Work.* London: Macmillan.
Steller, M. & Boychuk,T. (1992) Children as witnesses in sexual abuse cases: Investigative interview and assessment techniques. In H. Dent & R. Flin (Eds), *Children as Witnesses.* Chichester: Wiley. pp.47–71.
Suvannathat, C. (1985) Past, present and future directions for Asian child rearings: A synthesis chapter. In C. Suvannathat, D. Bhanthumnavin, L. Bhuapirom & D.M. Keats (Eds), *Handbook of Asian Child Development and Child Rearing Practices.* Bangkok: Behavioral Science Research Institute. pp.407–415.
Tesch, R. (1991), Software for qualitative researchers: Analysis needs and program capabilities. In N. G. Fielding & R.M. Lee (Eds), *Using Computers in Qualitative Research.* London: Sage. pp.16–37.

Thomas, D.R. (1986) Culture and ethnicity: Maintaining the difference. *Australian Journal of Psychology, 38,* 371–380.

Thomas, T. (1999) Stress, coping, and the mental health of older Vietnamese migrants. *Australian Psychologist, 34,* (2), 82–86.

Waring, T. (1992) The human factor: Trauma and counselling. In T. Housley (Ed.), *Disaster Management, Planning and Recovery.* Sydney: Housley Computer Communications. pp.240–256.

Weinreich, P. (1999) Ethnic identity and enculturation/acculturation. In J.-C. Lasry, J. Adair & K. Dion (Eds), *Latest Contributions to Cross-Cultural Psychology.* (pp.135–148) Lisse: Swets & Zeitlinger.

Wernimont, P.F. & Campbell, J.P. (1968) Signs, samples and criteria. *Journal of Applied Psychology, 52,* 372–376.

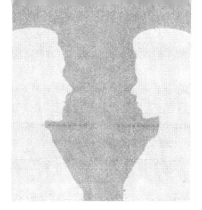

INDEX